COAST TO COAST
WALK

HILLSIDE GUIDES - ACROSS THE NORTH

Long Distance Walks
•COAST TO COAST WALK   •DALES WAY   •CUMBRIA WAY
•WESTMORLAND WAY •FURNESS WAY •LADY ANNE'S WAY •PENDLE WAY
•BRONTE WAY   •CALDERDALE WAY   •NIDDERDALE WAY

Circular Walks - Yorkshire Dales
•WHARFEDALE   •MALHAMDALE   •SWALEDALE   •NIDDERDALE
•THREE PEAKS   •WENSLEYDALE   •HOWGILL FELLS
•HARROGATE & the WHARFE VALLEY   •RIPON & LOWER WENSLEYDALE

Hillwalking - Lake District
•LAKELAND FELLS - SOUTH   •LAKELAND FELLS - EAST
•LAKELAND FELLS - NORTH   •LAKELAND FELLS - WEST

Circular Walks - Lancashire/North West
•BOWLAND   •PENDLE & the RIBBLE   •WEST PENNINE MOORS
•ARNSIDE & SILVERDALE   •LUNESDALE

Circular Walks - North Pennines
•TEESDALE   •EDEN VALLEY   •ALSTON & ALLENDALE

Circular Walks - North East Yorkshire
•NORTH YORK MOORS, SOUTHERN   •HOWARDIAN HILLS

Circular Walks - South Pennines
•ILKLEY MOOR   •BRONTE COUNTRY
•CALDERDALE   •SOUTHERN PENNINES

Short Scenic Walks - Full Colour Pocket Guides
Yorkshire Dales
•UPPER WHARFEDALE   •LOWER WHARFEDALE   •MALHAMDALE
•UPPER WENSLEYDALE   •LOWER WENSLEYDALE   •SWALEDALE
•NIDDERDALE   •SEDBERGH & DENTDALE
•RIBBLESDALE   •INGLETON & the WESTERN DALES
Northern England
•HARROGATE & KNARESBOROUGH   •ILKLEY & the WASHBURN VALLEY
•AIRE VALLEY   •AMBLESIDE & LANGDALE   •BORROWDALE
•BOWLAND   •AROUND PENDLE   •RIBBLE VALLEY

*Send for a detailed current catalogue and price list
and also visit www.hillsidepublications.co.uk*

WALKING COUNTRY

COAST TO COAST WALK

Paul Hannon

Hillside

ISBN 978-1-907626-01-2

TO
My good companion Pete and the Silver Jubilee Coast to Coasters
And my invaluable best companion Lisa, a third of a century later...

Whilst the author has walked and researched all the route for the
purposes of this guide, no responsibility can be accepted for any
unforeseen circumstances encountered while following it. The
publisher would appreciate information regarding material changes.

Cover: Robin Hood's Bay; Swaledale; Ullswater; Blakey Ridge
Back cover: Swaledale; Haystacks; Littlebeck
Page One: At Anglers' Crag, Ennerdale Water
Page Three: Sundial at Keld
(Paul Hannon/Hillslides Picture Library)

The route is based upon 'A Coast to Coast Walk' by A Wainwright,
originally published by Westmorland Gazette 1972
The sketch maps are based upon Ordnance Survey
1947 One-Inch maps and 1900-1930 1:10,560 maps,
redrawn to include up-to-date, on the ground research

Printed by Steffprint
Unit 5, Keighley Industrial Park
Royd Ings Avenue
Keighley
West Yorkshire
BD21 4DZ

CONTENTS

Brotherswater and Fairfield from the path to Angle Tarn

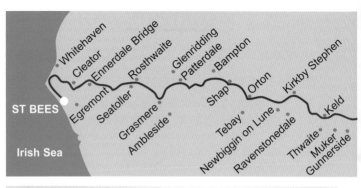

St Bees Head

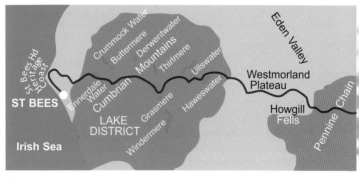

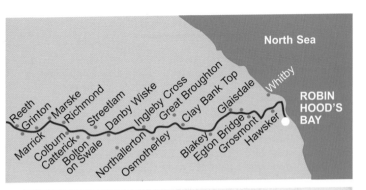

North Sea

Reeth Grinton Marske Richmond Streetlam Danby Wiske Ingleby Cross Great Broughton Clay Bank Top Glaisdale Whitby

Marrick Colburn Catterick Bolton on Swale Northallerton Osmotherley Blakey Egton Bridge Grosmont Hawsker

ROBIN HOOD'S BAY

Robin Hood's Bay

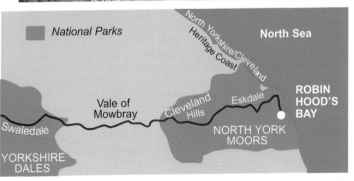

National Parks

North Yorkshire/Cleveland Heritage Coast

North Sea

ROBIN HOOD'S BAY

Vale of Mowbray

Cleveland Hills

Eskdale

Swaledale

NORTH YORK MOORS

YORKSHIRE DALES

INTRODUCTION

Coast to Coast - the very name is inspiring, from clifftop to clifftop across our small but perfectly formed land, magnificent strides through some of the grandest scenery in the North. The mountains of Lakeland, the Pennine uplands, glorious Swaledale, the Cleveland Hills, and Eskdale and the North York Moors, so much magic in so little space! Little wonder that walkers relish its clarion call, and enthuse ever afterwards over its finest moments.

As originator of the Coast to Coast Walk in the early 1970s, the late A Wainwright was a hallowed name to tens of thousands of hill-walkers through his previous guidebooks. Subsequently the media transformed him into a household name, and the end result is that few people have not now heard of the Coast to Coast Walk. Having devised the entire route himself through his personal cross-section of the North's best walking country, it may be regarded as his finest hour, and as such is just that little bit special.

As a long-standing admirer of the walk's creator it gave particular satisfaction to produce, in 1992, the first new guide to the route since Wainwright's masterpiece. At that time the original work had not kept pace with the countless changes of two decades: the route's thousands of walkers badly needed re-directing onto the right paths with up-to-date supporting information. This pleasurable task was savoured as a personal tribute to Wainwright, a more practical memorial than a cairn or a re-named tarn. Wainwright was seldom less than a perfectionist, and if this guide falls short of his exacting standards, he would surely have been happy to see his followers on the right track.

Compiled in 2010, this fully revised edition incorporates the many changes of previous decades, from inevitable ones such as disappearing hedgerows and new stiles and waymarking to those brought about by path diversions, creations, or to accommodate the wishes of landowners. Various suggestions for local alternatives are included here, though the guide adheres to the original route where it remains in common use. On numerous occasions, previous editions of this guide introduced the walk to logically sited public footpaths to avoid entirely unnecessary and potentially dangerous road walking: some have now been adopted as the accepted route, as well as several other very useful improvements, notably at Sunbiggin Tarn and in the Vale of Mowbray.

PLANNING THE WALK

The Coast to Coast Walk runs from St Bees on the Cumbrian coast to Robin Hood's Bay on the Yorkshire coast, a distance of some 192 miles. Several of Wainwright's original 12 stages have proved a little too daunting for many: within these pages the walk has been divided into 16 stages for practical purposes, but as the sketch maps and mileages are continuous this will have little effect on your own chosen route. Most people will aim to complete the walk within a fortnight's holiday, which with a spare day or two will accommodate these stages. However, several are short enough or easy enough to merge, and the best options for saving odd days are as follows (route alternatives within each section are included in their respective introduction):

- Merge Stages 3 and 4, short-cutting Grasmere (a shame though)
- Merge Stages 5, 6 and 7 into two by replacing Burnbanks and Orton with Shap
- Merge Stages 8, 9 and 10 into two by taking the valley route rather than the moors route through Swaledale: several villages offer a break
- Merge Stages 14, 15 and 16 into two long days by substituting Rosedale Head and Grosmont with Glaisdale

Unless planning to come out of season it is vital to book in advance to ensure a bed at the end of each day. Campers are well catered for, on the whole, and are more likely to get by on a casual day to day basis. Accommodation ranges from plush hotels by way of pubs, guesthouses, youth hostels, bunkbarns, camping barns and campsites to a farmer's field for your tent.

At St Bees:
Rucksack packed,
ready for off...

The popularity of the walk has led to a plethora of support services created specifically for Coast to Coast walkers. If you opt to haul your full rucksack around with you then you'll soon realise that you're in a minority. Most walkers take advantage of baggage carriers to ferry heavy packs between overnight halts, leaving you to stroll along with a light daypack - after all, it is a holiday! Happy experience of the Sherpa Van service confirms the carriers fulfil an invaluable role. Numerous enterprises also arrange accommodation packages through which the entire walk can be booked in one fell swoop, in some cases still selecting your own overnight stops.

Access to the start and finish of the route is not too difficult. St Bees is on the Cumbrian coast railway, and its station connects most easily with Carlisle (north) and also Barrow, for Lancaster (south). Robin Hood's Bay long since lost its station, but is served by the Whitby-Scarborough bus which links with railway stations in both towns. If heading southwards, then the longer bus ride to Scarborough will find you with a better service to the main line at York.

Finally, bear in mind that coffee table books and television largely portray only the glamorous side of a long-distance walk, giving little mention of blood, sweat and tears. Weather (incessant

rain, or believe it or not, heatwaves), blisters, or simply the effects of a heavy pack day after day can all contribute to a sad experience. Seasoned hillwalkers should have little difficulty in taking the Coast to Coast Walk in their stride, but the less experienced might wish to ensure they become more experienced before they venture onto a multi-day trek such as this one: the Northern Hills are very much in evidence!

The old streets of Robin Hood's Bay

THE ROUTE GUIDE

The main body of the book is a detailed guide to the walk, extending from page 16 through to page 155. It divides into sixteen sections, each having its own introduction quickly located by reference to the contents on page 5. Each includes a gradient profile (vertical scale is greatly exaggerated!) and summary of the walking, with suggestions for alternatives that can be plotted from OS maps. A continuous strip-map runs through the guide, accompanied by a narrative of the route. Remaining space is then devoted to notes and images of the many features of interest encountered along the way, such as this friendly chap at Moor Row.

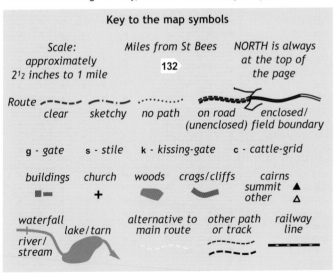

Key to the map symbols

Scale: approximately 2½ inches to 1 mile

Miles from St Bees

132

NORTH is always at the top of the page

Route ————— clear   —·—·— sketchy   ·········· no path   on road (unenclosed)   enclosed/ field boundary

g - gate   **s** - stile   **k** - kissing-gate   **c** - cattle-grid

buildings   church   woods   crags/cliffs   cairns
summit ▲
other △

waterfall   lake/tarn   river/ stream

alternative to main route

other path or track

railway line

11

USEFUL FACILITIES

This a general guide: about the only thing that might not change almost overnight is the location of railway stations! (a Post office is usually, but not quite always, a shop as well, a cafe could be basic refreshments, and a bus could be once a week)

	Hotel/B&B	Hostel/Barn	Camping	Bus service	Rail station	Pub	Post office	Shop	WC	Phone box	Cafe
St Bees	•		•	•	•	•	•	•	•	•	•
Sandwith	•	•				•				•	
Moor Row				•						•	•
Cleator	•			•		•		•		•	•
Ennerdale Bridge	•		•	•		•				•	
Gillerthwaite		•	•								
Black Sail Hut		•									•
Honister Pass		•		•					•	•	•
Seatoller	•		•	•		•			•	•	
Rosthwaite	•	•	•	•		•			•	•	•
Stonethwaite	•	•	•	•		•			•	•	•
Grasmere	•	•		•		•	•	•	•	•	•
Patterdale	•	•	•	•		•		•	•	•	•
Glenridding	•	•		•		•	•	•	•	•	•
Burnbanks				•					•		
Bampton	•			•		•	•		•		•
Bampton Grange	•			•		•			•		
Shap	•	•	•	•		•	•	•	•	•	•
Orton	•		•			•	•		•	•	•
Raisbeck	•		•						•		
Newbiggin on Lune	•	•	•	•						•	•
Ravenstonedale	•			•		•		•	•		
Kirkby Stephen	•	•	•	•	•	•	•	•	•	•	•
Raven Seat											•
Keld	•	•	•	•		•			•	•	•
Muker	•		•	•		•		•	•	•	•
Gunnerside	•			•		•			•	•	•
Low Row	•	•	•	•		•	•		•	•	•
Reeth	•	•	•	•		•	•	•	•	•	•
Grinton	•	•		•		•			•	•	
Marrick	•		•							•	•
Marske	•								•		

12

	Hotel/B&B	Hostel/Barn	Camping	Bus service	Rail station	Pub	Post office	Other shop	WC	Phone box	Cafe
Richmond	•	•	•	•		•	•	•	•	•	•
Colburn			•	•		•	•	•		•	
Catterick Bridge	•		•	•		•				•	
Brompton on Swale	•	•	•	•		•	•	•		•	
Scorton	•			•		•	•			•	•
Bolton on Swale			•	•						•	
Ellerton on Swale	•									•	
Danby Wiske	•		•	•		•				•	
Oaktree Hill	•	•	•	•							
Ingleby Arncliffe/X	•		•	•		•		•		•	•
Osmotherley	•	•	•	•		•	•	•		•	•
Swainby	•		•	•		•			•	•	
Carlton Bank								•	•	•	
Carlton	•		•	•		•				•	
Cringle Moor	•		•								
Great Broughton	•		•	•		•	•			•	
Chop Gate	•		•	•		•		•		•	
Farndale Head	•	•	•			•				•	
Westerdale	•	•				•				•	
Blakey/Rosedale Hd	•		•	•		•					
Glaisdale	•		•	•	•	•			•	•	
Egton Bridge	•		•	•	•	•			•	•	
Grosmont	•		•	•	•	•	•		•	•	•
Littlebeck	•		•							•	
Hawsker	•		•	•		•		•		•	•
Robin Hood's Bay	•	•	•	•		•	•	•	•	•	•

MAPS COVERING THE WALK

Ordnance Survey Landranger maps (1:50,000 scale)
•89 •90 •91 •92 •98 •99 •93 •94

Ordnance Survey Explorer maps (1:25,000 scale)
•303 •OL4 •OL7 •OL5 •OL19 •OL30 •304 •302 •OL26 •OL27

Harvey Maps (1:40,000 scale)
•Coast to Coast West •Coast to Coast East

Footprint Maps from Stirling Surveys (1:50,000 scale)
•Coast to Coast West •Coast to Coast East

USEFUL CONTACTS

COAST TO COAST SERVICES

Sherpa Van Project (baggage/transport/accommodation)
29 The Green, Richmond DL10 4RG
• 0871-520 0124   www.sherpavan.com

The Coast to Coast Packhorse (baggage/transport)
Chestnut House, Crosby Garrett, Kirkby Stephen CA17 4PR
• 017683-71777   www.c2cpackhorse.co.uk

Discovery Travel (walks accommodation)
York Hub, Pope's Head Court, Peter Lane, York YO1 8SU
• 01904-632226   www.discoverytravel.co.uk

Brigantes Walking Holidays (baggage/walks accommodation)
Rookery Cottage, Kirkby Malham, Skipton BD23 4BX
• 01729-830463   www.brigantesenglishwalks.com

Contours Walking Holidays (walks accommodation)
Gramyre, 3 Berrier Road, Greystoke, Cumbria CA11 0UB
• 017684-80451   www.contours.co.uk

Mrs Whitehead's Coast to Coast B&B Accommodation Guide
Castle Hill Books, 1 Castle Hill, Richmond DL10 4QP • 01748-824243

General reference: www.coasttocoastguides.co.uk

ORGANISATIONS

The Ramblers
2nd Floor, Camelford House, 87-90 Albert Embankment, London SE1 7TW
• 020-7339 8500   www.ramblers.org.uk

Friends of the Lake District
Murley Moss, Oxenholme Road, Kendal LA9 7SS • 01539-720788
www.fld.org.uk

Yorkshire Dales Society
Town Hall, Cheapside, Settle BD24 9EJ • 01729-825600
www.yds.org.uk

North Yorkshire Moors Association
Secretary: 2 High Street, Castleton, Whitby YO21 2DA
www.north-yorkshire-moors.org.uk

NATIONAL PARK AUTHORITIES

Lake District National Park Authority
Murley Moss, Oxenholme Road, Kendal LA9 7RL • 01539-7224555

Yorkshire Dales National Park Authority
Colvend, Hebden Road, Grassington BD23 5LB • 01756-751600

North York Moors National Park Authority
The Old Vicarage, Bondgate, Helmsley YO6 5BP • 01439-770657

NATIONAL PARK/TOURIST INFORMATION – ON OR NEAR THE WALK

Market Hall, Market Place, Whitehaven CA28 7JG • 01946-598914
12 Main Street, Egremont CA22 2DW • 01946-820693
The Moot Hall, Market Square, Keswick CA12 5JR • 017687-72645
Central Buildings, Market Cross, Ambleside LA22 9BS • 015394-32582
Main Car Park, Glenridding Penrith CA11 0PA • 017684-82414
Market Street, Kirkby Stephen CA17 4QN • 017683-71199
Hudson House, Reeth DL11 6TB • 01748-884059
Friary Gardens, Victoria Road, Richmond DL10 4AJ • 01748-828742
The Applegarth, Northallerton DL7 8LZ • 01609-776864
Moors Centre, Lodge Lane, Danby Whitby YO21 2NB • 01439-772737
Langborne Road, Whitby YO21 1YN • 01723-383636

PUBLIC TRANSPORT

National Rail Enquiries
• 08457-484950
www.nationalrailenquiries.org.uk

Traveline www.traveline.org.uk
• 0871-200 2233 874 (Cumbria)
• 0871-200 2233 883 (Nth Yorks)

Ullswater

St Bees to Ennerdale Bridge

DISTANCE 14¹⁄₂ miles (23km)   *ASCENT 1900 feet/580m*

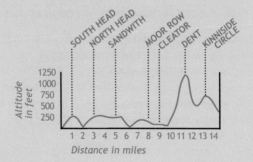

Distance in miles

The opening day offers three well-defined sections, though in this sandwich the filling is the least appetising part. That rare creature the Cumbrian clifftop provides a splendid introduction to the walk, several airy miles of tall sea cliffs putting you in the perfect frame of mind for a near-200 mile walk. On leaving the coast there follow several interesting but unexciting miles, as a corner of the old West Cumberland industrial belt is traversed. Ahead, however, are the hills, and beyond Cleator the unassuming little fell of Dent, is, despite its afforestation, a foretaste of Lakeland.

Alternatives, other than short-cuts, are few: this is a more circuitous day than most, and an obvious bee-line for Ennerdale Bridge can be plotted. Other than a path climbing from St Bees to Loughrigg Farm, however, road walking dominates the short-cut. The two great natural features of the walk are both time-consuming, though only in desperation should St Bees Head be omitted: there's nothing like it for a long time! If flagging, the back road from Cleator to Ennerdale Bridge avoids Dent.

When the great moment arrives and you're stood on the sea wall facing the Irish Sea, complete the first task by dipping at least a toe into its waters before making for the cliffs: modern tradition also suggests you pick up a small pebble to carry to the North Sea! The sea wall ends abruptly where a footbridge crosses Rottington Beck. Ascent to the clifftops is by way of a steep flight of fading wooden steps, after which it's easy going up aloft for an inspiring introduction to the Coast to Coast Walk.

ST BEES is an intriguing village, rich in historical interest but also attractive in its own right, even without its backdrop of the headland. The name of St Bega is the recurring link from earliest times to the present day. The Priory Church gives her shared billing in its dedication, for back in 650 AD this Irish princess established a nunnery here. Destroyed by the Danes, the site was given new life as a priory in about 1120 by Benedictine monks from York. The strikingly beautiful west doorway remains intact from the priory's early years. Also famous is the grammar school, which itself dates back over four centuries. Aside from the obligatory modern attachments, the heart of the village is a long, straggling main street. The village has a Post office/shop, cafe, hotel, restaurants and pubs. The railway arrived from Whitehaven in 1849, and as a fortunate survivor it plays an important role on the Cumbrian Coast line 'way out west'.

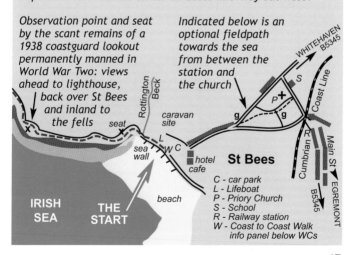

Observation point and seat by the scant remains of a 1938 coastguard lookout permanently manned in World War Two: views ahead to lighthouse, back over St Bees and inland to the fells

Indicated below is an optional fieldpath towards the sea from between the station and the church

WHITEHAVEN B5345

Coast Line

Rottington Beck

seat

caravan site

sea wall

L

W

C

hotel

cafe

S

P +

g

g

R

Cumbrian

Main St

B5345

EGREMONT

St Bees

IRISH SEA

THE START

beach

C - car park
L - Lifeboat
P - Priory Church
S - School
R - Railway station
W - Coast to Coast Walk
    info panel below WCs

After a lengthy spell on the seaward side of the fence on South Head, the path transfers over for a steady drop to the major inlet of Fleswick Bay. The path descends to within a few feet of sea level before regaining height for the longer march over North Head, though many will be tempted by a short path onto the shore. Here are cliffs, flowers, birds, caves, waterworn rocks, a dazzling array of smooth pebbles - and of course the sea.

Forging on below the lighthouse and alongside the lookout, the path is returned in dramatic fashion to the clifftop around the point of North Head. A carpet of springtime bluebells decorate this stage: ahead, Saltom Bay laps the Whitehaven shoreline, with the harbour entrance visible. Very soon the path re-crosses to the safer side of the fence, crossing a field to a kissing-gate to resume above higher level 'inland' cliffs. This curious feature is replicated on several occasions just here, including a section where the path itself runs a narrow course between rock walls before resuming between clifftop and fieldside.

ST BEES HEAD is the grandest feature on the Cumbrian coast, nature's answer to the monstrosity a few miles south. It is also the westernmost point in England outside of the South-west peninsula. Its mighty sandstone cliffs harbour a rich tangle of flowers, while birdlife from guillemots to kittiwakes is recognized in importance by an RSPB reserve. Observation points on North Head permit easy viewing of the nesting ledges.

Looking very close on a clear day, the Isle of Man is replaced by the Galloway Hills as North Head is turned

Saltom Bay

North Head

coastguard lookout

St Bees Head

IRISH SEA

seat on knoll

3

SANDWITH

St Bees Lighthouse

REMEMBER! the 'dangerous cliffs' warning signs aren't for decoration

Britain's last coal-powered lighthouse was built in 1822, and its keepers were usurped by computers in 1987

At 462ft/141m this is the highest point on the headland → x

2

Fleswick Bay

1

South Head

Left: St Bees Lighthouse and Fleswick Bay

Below: North Head

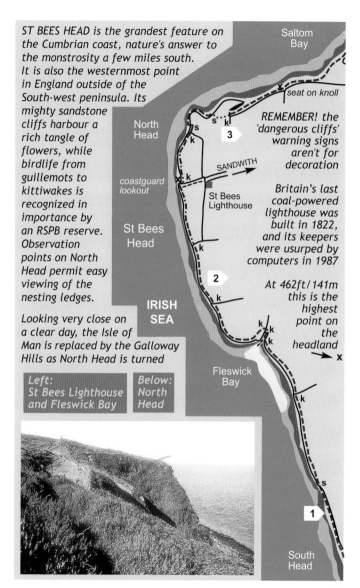

19

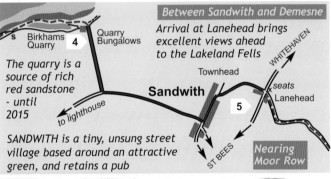

Between Sandwith and Demesne

Arrival at Lanehead brings excellent views ahead to the Lakeland Fells

Birkhams Quarry

4

Quarry Bungalows

WHITEHAVEN

Townhead

seats

Lanehead

Sandwith

The quarry is a source of rich red sandstone - until 2015

to lighthouse

5

ST BEES

SANDWITH is a tiny, unsung street village based around an attractive green, and retains a pub

Nearing Moor Row

The end of the cliff walk comes as a shock on emerging at Birkhams Quarry. A broad, diverted path runs between cliffs and quarry to approach the cottages: here turn inland on a lane part sunken between hedgerows, then left at a junction with the lighthouse road to enter Sandwith by the green. Turn left, curving right up past the Dog & Partridge to a junction at Lanehead. Cross straight over to run the full length of a gem of a green byway to Demesne. Turn right through the farmyard and out along a rough track onto the B5345 Whitehaven-St Bees road. Cross straight over and along the farm road to Bell House. Keep on past it to a cattle-grid on a brow, with a splendid prospect ahead. As the track forks on descent, bear right to a gate, then trend left down a thinner branch to the right-hand of two gates, keeping on down above a hedgerow to a railway underpass.

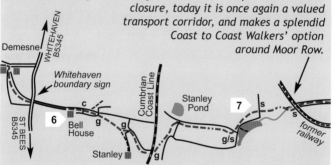

The enthusiastically developed WEST CUMBRIA CYCLE PATH now occupies this former railway. The defunct line was part of the Whitehaven, Cleator & Egremont Junction Railway, at one time a veritable labyrinth of tracks serving the area, in particular its assorted industry. In use only as a mineral line prior to its total closure, today it is once again a valued transport corridor, and makes a splendid Coast to Coast Walkers' option around Moor Row.

On the other side bear left across a flat pasture to a footbridge in the far corner, over which shrubbery encloses hidden Stanley Pond. A faint path crosses a long enclosure towards a wood, escaping by a gate/stile on the left before swinging right (ignore a track into trees) to climb two fields to another railway underpass. Now the West Cumbria Cycle Path, you might take steps on the other side to join it here (going east) or a little further into Moor Row, with me. A hedgerowed way climbs to meet the A595 Whitehaven-Egremont road.

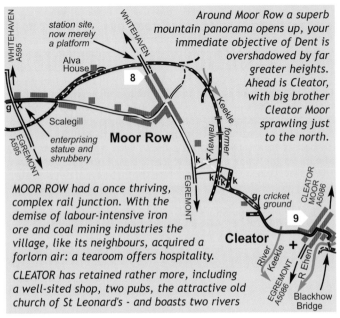

station site, now merely a platform

Alva House

8

WHITEHAVEN A595

WHITEHAVEN

Scalegill

enterprising statue and shrubbery

Moor Row

g

EGREMONT A595

Keekle

former railway

k

k

k K k

EGREMONT

g cricket ground

9

CLEATOR MOOR A5086

Cleator

+

River Keekle

R Ehen

EGREMONT A5086

Blackhow Bridge

Around Moor Row a superb mountain panorama opens up, your immediate objective of Dent is overshadowed by far greater heights. Ahead is Cleator, with big brother Cleator Moor sprawling just to the north.

MOOR ROW had a once thriving, complex rail junction. With the demise of labour-intensive iron ore and coal mining industries the village, like its neighbours, acquired a forlorn air: a tearoom offers hospitality.

CLEATOR has retained rather more, including a well-sited shop, two pubs, the attractive old church of St Leonard's - and boasts two rivers

Dent from Cleator

Cross with care to a highly appropriate sculpture and novel hedge, and along Scalegill Road into Moor Row. While the original route sticks to the road through the village, preferably join the cycleway by going left on a drive just before the old rail bridge: at the houses a path takes over to join the surfaced cycleway, going left under a bridge at the station site to a former junction just beyond. Bear right and a few steps further remain on the main way going left for a grand stroll through exuberant greenery above the River Keekle. When the old route joins from the right opposite another appropriate edifice, a path drops left off the line and down to cross an access track. Across a field a hedge-rowed path is followed right towards Cleator, emerging by a cricket ground at 'Wainwright Passage'. An access road leads out over the Keekle to enter Cleator's main street alongside the church.

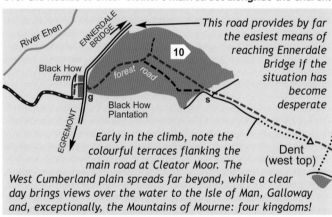

This road provides by far the easiest means of reaching Ennerdale Bridge if the situation has become desperate

Early in the climb, note the colourful terraces flanking the main road at Cleator Moor. The West Cumberland plain spreads far beyond, while a clear day brings views over the water to the Isle of Man, Galloway and, exceptionally, the Mountains of Mourne: four kingdoms!

Go left a short way to a shop in a terrace, and turn down Kiln Brow opposite. At the bottom go right along Millers Walk to Blackhow Bridge over the Ehen, from where a hedgerowed cart track climbs left. First stage of the ascent of Dent, this works up the slope to Black How Farm, passing round the nearside of the buildings to emerge onto a road. Opposite, a forest road doubles back up to the left through Black How Plantation. When some height has been gained a guidepost at a clearing sends a path 50 paces left to resume a parallel climb on far more accommodating terrain. The pleasant path soon breaks free of the plantations, maintaining its straight line to arrive at the big cairn atop Dent.

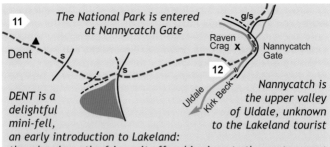

The National Park is entered
at Nannycatch Gate

g/s

Raven
Crag **x**   Nannycatch
Gate

Dent — s

12

Uldale   Kirk Beck

DENT is a
delightful
mini-fell,

Nannycatch is
the upper valley
of Uldale, unknown
to the Lakeland tourist

an early introduction to Lakeland:
though only on the fringe, it offers big views to the westernmost
fells, at the heart of which is the deep enclave of Ennerdale to
be penetrated on the next stage. This is a superb wilderness
panorama stretching from Hopegill Head through Grasmoor,
High Stile, Pillar and the Scafells to the Black Combe ridge.

This is only the traditional summit and not the true one, which is found across the marshy depression to the east. Possessing the most diminutive of cairns, it turns its back on the plain in favour of its grandstand setting for Lakeland's western skyline. Descend to a fence-stile and down a broad path through a felled plantation, over a minor crossroads to reach a junction with a forest road. Go left, and within a minute take a ladder-stile in the fence ahead, onto the contrastingly open eastern shoulder of the fell. A clear path runs to the far end to drop uncomfortably steeply to Nannycatch Beck. Turn left on the path through this narrow and immensely pleasant little valley, over a brace of footbridges and a stile at Nannycatch Gate.

Passing below gorse-draped Flatfell Screes up to the left, the beck fades but the clear path bears right beneath a small craggy knoll to work steadily up towards the open fell road. A branch path doubles back right to visit Kinniside Stone Circle, which well merits an inspection: if keeping on to the end, then turn briefly right on a farm road to join the fell road. Go left on the road until it becomes enclosed at a cattle-grid. Here a path on the left escapes the tarmac on a splendid parallel course between hedgerows, crossing a farm drive en route to ultimately rejoin the road: this steady descent to Ennerdale Bridge enjoys the parade of mountains as a finale to this stage. At Lanefoot a section on open ground opposite leads closer to the village, with one final short side path beyond a road junction.

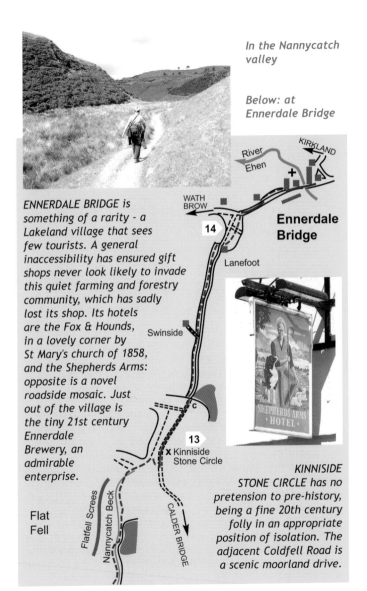

In the Nannycatch valley

Below: at Ennerdale Bridge

ENNERDALE BRIDGE is something of a rarity - a Lakeland village that sees few tourists. A general inaccessibility has ensured gift shops never look likely to invade this quiet farming and forestry community, which has sadly lost its shop. Its hotels are the Fox & Hounds, in a lovely corner by St Mary's church of 1858, and the Shepherds Arms: opposite is a novel roadside mosaic. Just out of the village is the tiny 21st century Ennerdale Brewery, an admirable enterprise.

River Ehen

KIRKLAND

WATH BROW

14

Ennerdale Bridge

Lanefoot

Swinside

c

13

x Kinniside Stone Circle

Flat Fell

Flatfell Screes

Nannycatch Beck

CALDER BRIDGE

KINNISIDE STONE CIRCLE has no pretension to pre-history, being a fine 20th century folly in an appropriate position of isolation. The adjacent Coldfell Road is a scenic moorland drive.

25

2

ENNERDALE BRIDGE TO ROSTHWAITE

DISTANCE 14$\frac{1}{2}$ miles (23km)   **ASCENT** 1800 feet/550m

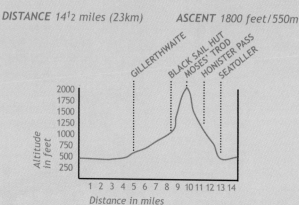

Another triple-section day comprising lakeshore, forest and mountainside as the length of Ennerdale precedes a crossing into Borrowdale. The opening miles are a splendid ramble along the southern shore of Ennerdale Water. While the higher reaches of the dale are draped in forestry, progress is rapid on a broad track giving improving glimpses up to the surrounding fells. Beyond Black Sail Hut the open air might have come off a prescription as, faced by high-walled mountains, the inevitable climb brings fresh views and a long and varied descent on broad paths into Borrowdale by way of the bustling Honister slate mine.

There are no shorter alternatives, but several more adventurous routes out of Ennerdale involve serious fellwalking, best left to the experienced. The least arduous alternative climbs to Scarth Gap Pass, then onto Haystacks, continuing on further paths to Moses' Trod: this takes on poignancy in view of the great man's final resting place. Higher level options include the High Stile ridge lining the valley to the north. Variations near the outset use the north shore path and forest road to the head of the lake; and a forest road south of the river as far as the Pillar footbridge.

Leave the village by the Croasdale Road past the school, turning right for the lake where indicated on a zigzag road that expires upon crossing the River Ehen. Go left past a car park on a broad path to the foot of Ennerdale Water. Ignore the bridge on the outflow and turn right on the south shore footpath.

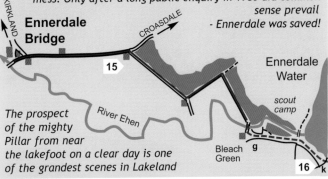

Westernmost of the English Lakes, ENNERDALE WATER has a lonely appeal rarely seen outside of Scotland. However, in 1978 a water authority plan to increase the amount of water currently being abstracted threatened to devastate the place, entailing large embankments, valuable farmland flooded, and a general mess. Only after a long public enquiry in 1980 did common sense prevail - Ennerdale was saved!

KIRKLAND

Ennerdale Bridge

CROASDALE

15

Ennerdale Water

scout camp

The prospect of the mighty Pillar from near the lakefoot on a clear day is one of the grandest scenes in Lakeland

River Ehen

Bleach Green

g

16 k

The start of the lakeside path, Ennerdale Water

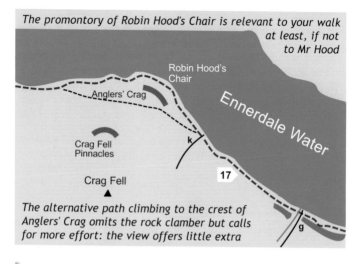

The promontory of Robin Hood's Chair is relevant to your walk at least, if not to Mr Hood

Robin Hood's Chair

Anglers' Crag

Ennerdale Water

Crag Fell Pinnacles

k

17

Crag Fell ▲

g

The alternative path climbing to the crest of Anglers' Crag omits the rock clamber but calls for more effort: the view offers little extra

ENNERDALE FOREST has sat as a dense, coniferous cloak between lake and dalehead since increased timber demands after the First World War saw it long suffocate the heart of Lakeland's remotest valley. While the Forestry Commission gradually created trails and implemented greater diversity of species, the 21st century has seen the start of a real transformation. In partnership with the water company and National Trust an innovative project has the objective of actively encouraging a 're-wilding' of the valley, where nature plays a greater part in enhancing its own landscape and habitats.

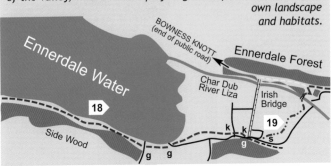

Opposite: Springtime in Ennerdale - looking across Ennerdale Water to Great Borne

The path runs undeviatingly along the length of the lake, almost always within reach of the water's edge. High up to the right in the early stages the fangs of Crag Fell Pinnacles tower menacingly above, while the individual highlight is the scrambly crossing of the base of Anglers' Crag, which plummets directly into the water (see page 1). The second half of the lakeside walk is through the wonderfully natural Side Wood, a section to be savoured in view of the imminent forest. From a gate at the end take the right-hand green way in this dead-flat strath at the lake-head. At the second wall a forest road is joined, presenting a choice of either going left with it to join the valley road (the simplest option), or following it into the forest, briefly, turning immediately left and within 100 paces left again to leave by a stile on the left. Aim half-right across the field for a footbridge over the River Liza, and from a tiny footbridge in the corner opposite, rise through trees to meet the firm valley road. Turn right to begin an unbroken march to the dalehead.

Five minutes beyond High Gillerthwaite the very demanding High Stile alternative departs from the valley as a sheep-droving break. A long, featureless climb to Red Pike is rewarded with a superb ridgewalk over High Stile, High Crag and Haystacks: a classic on a clear day, but with a heavy rucksack on your back, ... perhaps better left alone.

20

Ennerdale Forest

Low Gillerthwaite

High Gillerthwaite

River Liza

Black Sail Hut

The road passes by Low Gillerthwaite (a field centre) and High Gillerthwaite (a youth hostel) where it becomes stonier. A forest road forges on over a cattle-grid deep into the trees, at the same time as the high-level High Stile ridgewalk option takes advantage of the break on the left. Your route forges on through the forest, undeflected by lesser branches or forks. When the great mountains reveal themselves, outstanding is the increasingly powerful outline of Pillar Rock, high up to the right. The hard road eventually reaches the end of the forest, and as it swings down to the right, take the gate in front with a glimpse of Black Sail Hut, and even better, Great Gable, behind it. A track runs to the youth hostel just ahead. After a welcome sojourn in the open spaces of the dalehead overlooked by Pillar, Kirk Fell and the Gables, ignore the main path which runs down to a footbridge over the Liza: instead, within a couple of strides take a much thinner path contouring left, up-dale. This quickly becomes clearer to enjoy a splendid traverse through a hummocky landscape of drumlins (left by retreating glaciers) to reach the unmistakeable cleft of Loft Beck only yards above its merger with Tongue Beck.

Here departs the less demanding Haystacks alternative route. The path first makes for Scarth Gap Pass, then climbs a well-worn pilgrimage route onto the rugged little fell's colourful summit, then meandering by heathery knolls and tarns before climbing to rejoin the walk.

21 Ennerdale Forest

The RIVER LIZA runs a short, enigmatic course from the wild head of Ennerdale into the lake

forest road bridge

22

River Liza

Pillar footbridge

Note that as part of Ennerdale's re-wilding, various sections of forest on the map have been felled, giving more open views to the magnificent surround of fells

All who travel the Coast to Coast Walk will surely be aware that the mountain pool of Innominate Tarn on the charismatic upper contours of his favourite fell Haystacks was the location Wainwright chose to be scattered after his death which came in 1991. Sad to think people wanted to rename the tarn in his honour: it already carries an ironic name, and in any case the man himself would have cringed at the very idea. Anyway, spare a quiet moment or two as you climb out of Ennerdale.

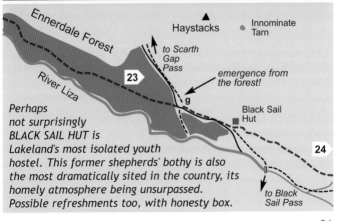

Ennerdale Forest

▲ Haystacks

● Innominate Tarn

to Scarth Gap Pass

23

emergence from the forest!

River Liza

g

Black Sail Hut

24

Perhaps not surprisingly BLACK SAIL HUT is Lakeland's most isolated youth hostel. This former shepherds' bothy is also the most dramatically sited in the country, its homely atmosphere being unsurpassed. Possible refreshments too, with honesty box.

to Black Sail Pass

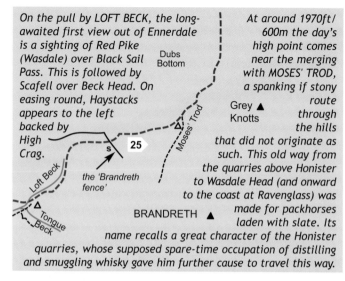

On the pull by LOFT BECK, the long-awaited first view out of Ennerdale is a sighting of Red Pike (Wasdale) over Black Sail Pass. This is followed by Scafell over Beck Head. On easing round, Haystacks appears to the left backed by High Crag.

Dubs Bottom

Grey ▲ Knotts

Moses' Trod

the 'Brandreth fence'

Loft Beck

Tongue Beck

BRANDRETH ▲

At around 1970ft/600m the day's high point comes near the merging with MOSES' TROD, a spanking if stony route through the hills that did not originate as such. This old way from the quarries above Honister to Wasdale Head (and onward to the coast at Ravenglass) was made for packhorses laden with slate. Its name recalls a great character of the Honister quarries, whose supposed spare-time occupation of distilling and smuggling whisky gave him further cause to travel this way.

On crossing Loft Beck a partly rebuilt path commences an immediate ascent of its bank, climbing steeply between heathery flanks. At the top a line of cairns escorts the path up easier ground, with Crummock Water and the Grasmoor Fells appearing across to the left: note also the sheer north wall of Haystacks, closer to hand. The Ennerdale boundary fence is crossed during its climb to Brandreth up to the right, while your path motors on its gentler way. Soon Moses' Trod will be espied contouring around the flank of Grey Knotts ahead, with your path set on a collision course with it. At the junction go left along its broad way, with the hollow of Dubs Bottom down to the left, and the Buttermere Valley making a memorable scene.

The Trod runs down to a major junction at the conspicuous remains of the Drum House. Go right on the dismantled tramway that runs unerringly down to the visitor centre on the summit of Honister Pass. The sudden population boom is tempered by the remarkable revelation of Honister Crag falling to the pass. Pass through the yard and a track beneath the youth hostel and a National Trust car park is the start of the old Honister road, which slants across the motor road and cleverly keeps generally clear of it as it spirals down to Borrowdale.

Haystacks from Dubs

Honister Crag

HONISTER PASS is one of Lakeland's better-known road passes. Part of its popularity is the ease with which it forms part of a circular tour from Keswick, a facility taken full advantage of before the advent of the motor car, when waggonette trips were hampered by passengers having to get out and walk the steeper sections! The former toll road gives escape from the traffic, being better graded and with spacious views over the mountains encircling the dalehead. While the hinterland of Honister Crag openly displays the scars of quarrying, its sombre face is riddled with tunnels and shafts from the hard days spent prising out slate. In a recent turnaround the mine once more operates, as a tourist venture but still winning small amounts of slate from the bowels of the earth. Underground tours can be enjoyed, while the affluent can take a via ferrata ('iron way'), alpine-style climb onto Fleetwith Pike.

A youth hostel sits on top of the pass

There is a also a café (more relevant!) and giftshop.

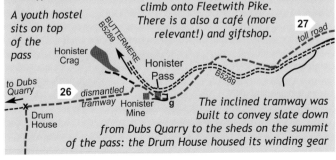

The inclined tramway was built to convey slate down from Dubs Quarry to the sheds on the summit of the pass: the Drum House housed its winding gear

33

On the old toll road   *Below: Borrowdale at Rosthwaite*

The track of the old road concludes through the enclosures above Seatoller, at the bottom doubling back into the top of the tiny village. Go left and leave by a stile at the end of the car park. Keeping right at an initial fork, a charming path runs on above the River Derwent, passing above a bridge over it and on through Johnny Wood. The final stage includes an intriguing rock scramble by the river, complete with iron safety chain! The path terminates at Longthwaite youth hostel. Cross the bridge on the Derwent, and a few yards up the road a path breaks off left behind cottages to run directly through the fields to Rosthwaite.

ROSTHWAITE is the focal point of the communities scattered round the head of Borrowdale, itself only a modest cluster of white-walled cottages and busy farms, hotels and a tea-room. The oaks of Johnny Wood and the rush of the Derwent make a fitting approach to the village. Borrowdale's church is to be found further along the Stonethwaite road.

At Seatoller

SEATOLLER'S cottages and farms huddle at the foot of Honister Pass. It has licensed premises at the Yew Tree, while the Keswick bus (open-topped, in summer, serving the wettest inhabited places in England!) terminates here.

Rosthwaite

KESWICK B5289

29

Longthwaite youth hostel

Johnny Wood

28

toll road

g/s

Seatoller

B5289

SEATHWAITE

River Derwent

The RIVER DERWENT is one of England's fairest, formed by the meeting of Styhead and Grains Gills and running a charmed course through Borrowdale into Derwentwater and ultimately Bassenthwaite Lake. Lined by trees and overlooked by an array of colourful fells, it doesn't get much better than this.

This is the road to Stonethwaite, a useful short-cut from Longthwaite if bound for the campsite or passing straight through Borrowdale

35

3

ROSTHWAITE TO GRASMERE

DISTANCE *9 miles (14¹⁄₂km)*   **ASCENT** *2230 feet/680m*

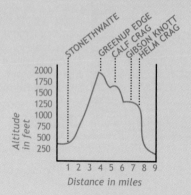

This is the first of two successive stages that walk against the grain, faced by a north-south ridge ranged against attempts at easterly progress. Clear paths make use of a pass which must be crossed at virtually the 2000ft contour: this does at least give the opportunity to incorporate a fascinating ridgewalk, even though its three summits are all lower than the pass that precedes them. The valley scenery at each end (Stonethwaite and Easedale) is matched only by the ultimate loveliness of the Vale of Grasmere.

Settling for Grasmere gives opportunity to incorporate higher summits into the day. With experience and weather on your side, options include Stonethwaite to Greenup Edge by way of Dock Tarn and Ullscarf, or leaving Greenup Edge for High Raise and Easedale Tarn. In contrast the direct route from Far Easedale Head down to Grasmere short-cuts the main route, an ideal option on a poor day but lovely nevertheless.

If determined to reach Patterdale from Rosthwaite, then instead of descending to valley level at Grasmere, consider dropping into Wythburn to meet the A591 above Thirlmere, then over Dunmail Raise to follow Raise Beck to Grisedale Tarn.

Leave Rosthwaite by an access road (Hazel Bank) off the main road on the north edge of the village, which runs to a bridge over Stonethwaite Beck. At a junction of pathways turn sharply right along a walled path that intermittently shadows the beck, becoming a field-path to run on past Stonethwaite Bridge.

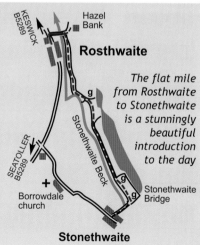

On the path into the Stonethwaite Valley past the idyllically sited campsite

STONETHWAITE is an archetypal Lakeland hamlet of white-walled cottages incorporating a country hotel (public bar) and low-key cottage refreshments. Borrowdale's church and school stand side by side on the cul-de-sac road leading to it.

The flat mile from Rosthwaite to Stonethwaite is a stunningly beautiful introduction to the day

Hazel Bank

Rosthwaite

KESWICK B5289

SEATOLLER B5289

Stonethwaite Beck

Borrowdale church

Stonethwaite Bridge

Stonethwaite

The arresting profile of EAGLE CRAG increases in grandeur during the long, easy march towards its base: by the time you gain Greenup Edge you'll be considerably more elevated than it!

The beck scenery in the vicinity of the Langstrath confluence is gorgeous: just over the footbridge is a deep pool beneath a steep-walled gorge

30 fold

Stonethwaite Beck

Galleny Force

Langstrath Beck

31

fold

Greenup Gill

LANGSTRATH is aptly named, for this 'long valley' extends for several miles from Lakeland's other Angle Tarn beneath the steep flanks of Bowfell in the very heart of the central massif of fells

Approaching Eagle Crag

▲ Eagle Crag

Langstrath Beck

Passing the birth of Stonethwaite Beck at the meeting of Langstrath Beck and Greenup Gill, the broad path forges on up the latter side-valley, now beneath Eagle Crag's dark wall. Further up the Greenup valley, the path leaves the final wall behind and rises to a knoll beneath the imposing Lining Crag. Through clusters of drumlins the path arrives at the foot of the crag, then climbs adventurously to its left on a restored path. The top of the crag is an amiable green knoll that few will pass without a detour, particularly as the next half-hour is much less auspicious: in any case, this is the place to bid farewell to Borrowdale. Above Lining Crag the gradients relent, and in moist surroundings the occasionally cairned path runs to the summit of the pass on Greenup Edge, marked by a line of old fenceposts. Exercise caution in poor visibility: the path can easily be lost as walkers have meandered widely across the moist plateau.

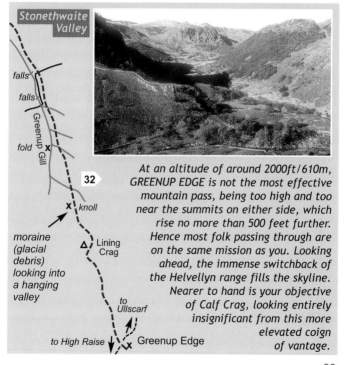

Stonethwaite Valley

falls

falls

Greenup Gill

fold x

32

x knoll

moraine (glacial debris) looking into a hanging valley

△ Lining Crag

to Ullscarf

to High Raise ↓ x Greenup Edge

At an altitude of around 2000ft/610m, GREENUP EDGE is not the most effective mountain pass, being too high and too near the summits on either side, which rise no more than 500 feet further. Hence most folk passing through are on the same mission as you. Looking ahead, the immense switchback of the Helvellyn range fills the skyline. Nearer to hand is your objective of Calf Crag, looking entirely insignificant from this more elevated coign of vantage.

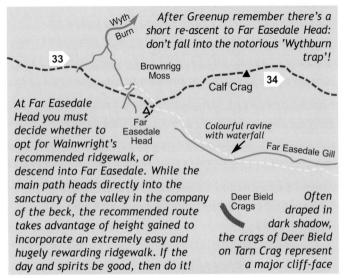

After Greenup remember there's a short re-ascent to Far Easedale Head: don't fall into the notorious 'Wythburn trap'!

Wyth Burn

33

Brownrigg Moss

Calf Crag

34

At Far Easedale Head you must decide whether to opt for Wainwright's recommended ridgewalk, or descend into Far Easedale. While the main path heads directly into the sanctuary of the valley in the company of the beck, the recommended route takes advantage of height gained to incorporate an extremely easy and hugely rewarding ridgewalk. If the day and spirits be good, then do it!

Far Easedale Head

Colourful ravine with waterfall

Far Easedale Gill

Deer Bield Crags

Often draped in dark shadow, the crags of Deer Bield on Tarn Crag represent a major cliff-face

From Greenup Edge the next pass at Far Easedale Head is in view several hundred feet below, beyond the intervening valley of Wythburn. The path descends sharply before swinging right across a marshy shelf, a variation left being little better than the main path, which gains the crest of the pass at some redundant fenceposts: see the note above regarding your choice here.

Along to the left a branch path climbs the undulating ridge to Calf Crag, a short-half mile distant, soon reaching its cairned top above a steep fall to Easedale. The path then winds down and along to the twin-cairned top of Gibson Knott: note that it does not slavishly adhere to the crest. The short descent to the next saddle, Bracken Hause, precedes a final pull to prominent Helm Crag waiting at the end, greeted by a knob of rock that marks the fell's true summit. The path runs along Helm Crag's fascinating crest to similarly appointed outcrops at the other end before commencing a pulsating descent towards the Vale of Grasmere. After a short drop the path runs onto a green knoll, where turn sharp right on a path that has replaced the original eroded one that continued down the ridge-end. This well-made substitute winds down more sedately to meet the valley path in Far Easedale, turning left to quickly become surfaced.

At 1761ft/537m CALF CRAG is the highest point on its ridge. On the ridgewalk beyond, the tops of the Langdale Pikes appear over an intervening ridge, while England's largest lake Windermere is much more distant.

Far Easedale Gill

35 ▷

▲
Gibson
Knott

Intermediate top GIBSON KNOTT attains 1384ft/422m, but is an unsung fell in the shadow of lower but more showy Helm Crag

A footbridge makes life easy at Stythwaite Steps

fold **x**

Stythwaite
Steps

Bracken
Hause

enclosure
dense with
hawthorn

▲
Helm
Crag

36

At 1328ft/405m the summit of HELM CRAG is a bewildering wonderland that repays careful exploration. The tilted rock tower pointing skyward is best known as the Howitzer, and demands an adventurous scramble to claim a true ascent of the fell. Grasmere's green vale shares the view with the great bulks of Helvellyn and Fairfield.

Easedale Beck

g

Brimmer
Head Farm

Looking back along the ridge from Helm Crag

Easedale

41

WILLIAM WORDSWORTH.
1850.
MARY WORDSWORTH
1859.

Grasmere

SARAH NELSON'S
Original Celebrated
GRASMERE
GINGERBREAD

The Easedale access road heads out through a field, has an encounter with Easedale Beck, and threads a long and pleasant winding course to Grasmere village. After crossing Goody Bridge (to which you shall return upon leaving), a parallel National Trust permissive path avoids the road to also reach the centre.

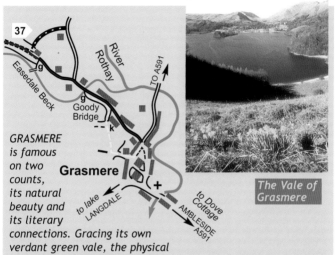

The Vale of Grasmere

GRASMERE is famous on two counts, its natural beauty and its literary connections. Gracing its own verdant green vale, the physical attributes leave nothing to the imagination. The River Rothay flows into Grasmere's own sheet of water, a quiet little mere disturbed only by rowing boats. Thronged with tourists from all corners of the globe, the village centre is supported by several hamlets along the main road. It is one of these, Town End, that hides Dove Cottage, iconic amongst William Wordsworth's Lakeland homes. Best known of the celebrated Lakes poets, he was Poet Laureate from 1843 to his death in 1850. He rests in St Oswald's churchyard, marked by the plainest of headstones. Other attractions at Grasmere include two famous annual events, the sports and the rushbearing. A legendary gingerbread shop, bookshop, and the Heaton Cooper gallery add to the more functional range of Post office, shops, pubs and teashops. The smaller of its two youth hostels served that role since 1931, but will probably have been closed by the time you read this.

4

GRASMERE TO PATTERDALE

DISTANCE 8^{1}2 miles (13^{1}2km)   *ASCENT 1725 feet / 525m*

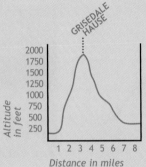

This section again walks against the grain, with another north-south ridge challenging easterly progress. However, today an excellent path is your guide across the Helvellyn-Fairfield ridge at little short of the 2000ft contour: the end of the day's climbing is marked by a wildly sited mountain tarn. The supremely lovely valley scenery of the Vale of Grasmere and Grisedale decorates each end, with the latter taking several delightful miles to welcome you down into the Ullswater district.

On this very confined stage, considerably higher mountains present the only alternative routes. In either case the main route is best followed to a path crossroads at the outflow of Grisedale Tarn, where a leisurely pause gives chance to consider the state of play. Your alternatives are now either a steady and relatively undemanding slant up onto Saint Sunday Crag, or the stiffer proposition of an ascent of mighty Helvellyn. This also leaves you with a more challenging descent to Patterdale, normally by way of Striding Edge or Swirral Edge: either of these ridges really requires a day of good weather - and don't forget you've got a serious fellwalk tomorrow, whatever the weather brings!

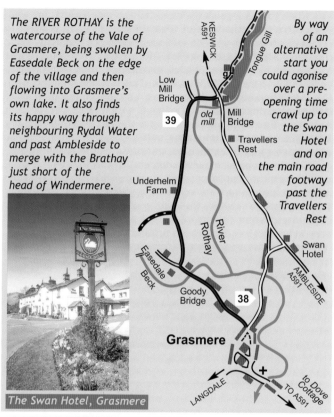

The RIVER ROTHAY is the watercourse of the Vale of Grasmere, being swollen by Easedale Beck on the edge of the village and then flowing into Grasmere's own lake. It also finds its happy way through neighbouring Rydal Water and past Ambleside to merge with the Brathay just short of the head of Windermere.

By way of an alternative start you could agonise over a pre-opening time crawl up to the Swan Hotel and on the main road footway past the Travellers Rest

KESWICK A591

Tongue Gill

Low Mill Bridge

old mill

39

Mill Bridge

Travellers Rest

Underhelm Farm

River Rothay

Easedale Beck

Swan Hotel

AMBLESIDE A591

Goody Bridge

38

Grasmere

LANGDALE

TO A591

to Dove Cottage

The Swan Hotel, Grasmere

Fairfield and Mill Bridge from Helm Crag

Depart Grasmere by heading back on Easedale Road, taking a side road right after Goody Bridge. Continue on to a junction and then right, up to the A591 at Mill Bridge. Cross the busy road and up an enclosed track opposite.

When the path gains the open fell a choice awaits, for well-worn paths run either side of Great Tongue, directly in front, to rejoin much higher up. The left-hand one is the old pony track, the other a better-used walkers' alternative. They meet under the eastern bluff of Seat Sandal, in readiness for gaining the top of Grisedale Hause at 1935ft/590m. This is a fine moment, with the tarn immediately below and the unremitting wall of Dollywaggon Pike dispelling many a notion of a detour over Helvellyn. Eminently more inviting is the noble profile of Saint Sunday Crag beyond the tarn's outflow, and if considering an alternative route to Patterdale, this presents the easier option.

For the moment however descend to the foot of the tarn, one of the most popular picnic spots in the district. Certainly the mountain atmosphere here is strong, even if none show their finest faces. On leaving, the main route crosses the outflow to begin the descent to Patterdale by way of Grisedale's long but easy miles, quickly passing the Brothers' Parting stone.

Fairfield from Hause Moss

Grisedale Tarn and Dollywaggon Pike, showing the descent path into Grisedale

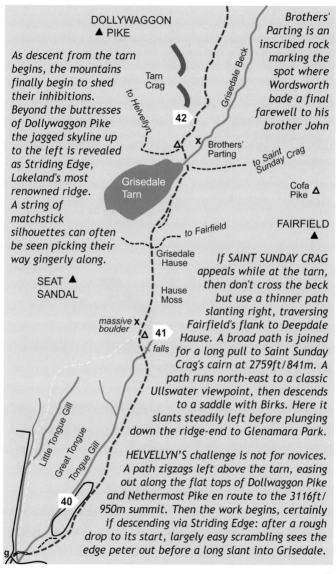

DOLLYWAGGON
▲ PIKE

As descent from the tarn begins, the mountains finally begin to shed their inhibitions. Beyond the buttresses of Dollywaggon Pike the jagged skyline up to the left is revealed as Striding Edge, Lakeland's most renowned ridge. A string of matchstick silhouettes can often be seen picking their way gingerly along.

Brothers' Parting is an inscribed rock marking the spot where Wordsworth bade a final farewell to his brother John

Tarn Crag

to Helvellyn

Grisedale Beck

42

△ ✗ Brothers' Parting

to Saint Sunday Crag

Grisedale Tarn

Cofa Pike △

to Fairfield

FAIRFIELD
▲

SEAT ▲
SANDAL

Grisedale Hause

Hause Moss

massive ✗
boulder

△ 41

✗ falls

If SAINT SUNDAY CRAG appeals while at the tarn, then don't cross the beck but use a thinner path slanting right, traversing Fairfield's flank to Deepdale Hause. A broad path is joined for a long pull to Saint Sunday Crag's cairn at 2759ft/841m. A path runs north-east to a classic Ullswater viewpoint, then descends to a saddle with Birks. Here it slants steadily left before plunging down the ridge-end to Glenamara Park.

Little Tongue Gill

Great Tongue

Tongue Gill

40

HELVELLYN'S challenge is not for novices. A path zigzags left above the tarn, easing out along the flat tops of Dollwaggon Pike and Nethermost Pike en route to the 3116ft/ 950m summit. Then the work begins, certainly if descending via Striding Edge: after a rough drop to its start, largely easy scrambling sees the edge peter out before a long slant into Grisedale.

g

The path descends to Ruthwaite Lodge, a little below which the alternative left branch crosses Ruthwaite Beck to remain on the north side of the valley, meeting the Striding Edge path at its foot to join the main route in the valley bottom. The main path continues down to a footbridge on Grisedale Beck and soon meets a wall, broadening to reach Elmhow via several pastures. The access road leads out along the valley floor to merge with other farm roads. While this narrow road drops down to the main road north of the village, part-way down a gate on the right points to a gate just above. Joined by the path coming down off Saint Sunday Crag go left, a finish through Glenamara Park's scattered trees drawing the day to a nice conclusion. Entering trees at Mill Moss, take the right fork to enter Patterdale by way of the WCs.

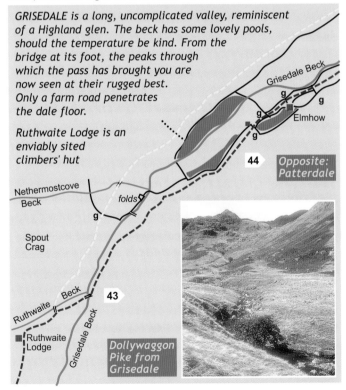

GRISEDALE is a long, uncomplicated valley, reminiscent of a Highland glen. The beck has some lovely pools, should the temperature be kind. From the bridge at its foot, the peaks through which the pass has brought you are now seen at their rugged best. Only a farm road penetrates the dale floor.

Ruthwaite Lodge is an enviably sited climbers' hut

Grisedale Beck

g

g

g

g

Elmhow

44　*Opposite: Patterdale*

Nethermostcove Beck

folds

g

Spout Crag

Ruthwaite Beck

43

Ruthwaite Lodge

Grisedale Beck

Dollywaggon Pike from Grisedale

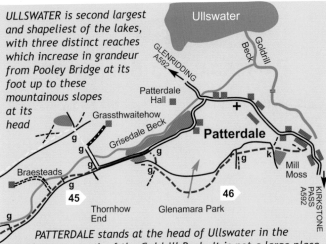

ULLSWATER is second largest and shapeliest of the lakes, with three distinct reaches which increase in grandeur from Pooley Bridge at its foot up to these mountainous slopes at its head

Ullswater

GLENRIDDING A592

Goldrill Beck

Patterdale Hall

Grassthwaitehow

Grisedale Beck

Patterdale

Braesteads

Mill Moss

KIRKSTONE PASS A592

45

46

Thornhow End

Glenamara Park

PATTERDALE stands at the head of Ullswater in the broad, green strath of the Goldrill Beck. It is not a large place, its various components being strung out along the A592. 'St Patrick's Dale' is an extremely popular resort, but its lack of size has helped preserve it from the excessive commercialism of other central Lakeland villages: boating and pony trekking are much-enjoyed peaceful pastimes. It has a couple of pubs and a Post office/shop. Although hemmed in by mountains, a motor road escapes north clinging to Ullswater's shore, and also south over the Kirkstone Pass towards Windermere and Ambleside.

5

PATTERDALE TO BURNBANKS

DISTANCE 11 miles (17½km)   **ASCENT** 2410 feet/735m

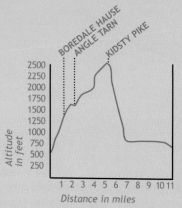

The vast High Street ridge stands between you and progress towards the Yorkshire coast, and a promising forecast will be much appreciated today. While High Street is the parent fell, a family of interlinking ridges spew forth from the skyline that is the summit of the Coast to Coast Walk. Boredale Hause and Angle Tarn break up the climb to the Straits of Riggindale, where a clear day gives first views east to Pennine country. From Kidsty Pike's precipitous crest the shore of Haweswater is soon alongside, and remains so for several miles virtually to the end of the stage. Bear in mind it's a short mile further to accommodation around Bampton.

The nature of intervening valleys drilling deep into the hills makes this the only logical route, other than enthusiasts adding further summits. If an alternative is sought due to poor weather, then a lower level, slightly longer walk follows Ullswater's shore to Howtown, taking a bridleway onto Moor Divock to descend to the Lowther valley north of Bampton. This is no poor alternative, but actually a very enjoyable and relatively easy one.

Leave the village by a side-road branching off just south of the White Lion, crossing Goldrill Bridge and swinging round to the left to terminate in a corner by the houses of Rooking. A gate on the right gains the open fell, and a path slants up to the right. At a fork below a seat keep to the lower path to rise steadily and quickly onto the broad, grassy saddle of Boredale Hause. When the going eases at a pair of cairns on a green plinth, cross the tiny beck above a sheepfold to a path winding up to the right.

The climb to the pass of BOREDALE HAUSE reveals increasingly breathtaking views over the Patterdale valley to the massif of Helvellyn and its lofty supporters: the head of Ullswater is a deep foreground. Further west is the Fairfield group, continuing to Red Screes crowning the fells around Kirkstonefoot. The higher path leads onto the true Boredale Hause, where the remains of a chapel resemble a ruinous sheepfold. Place Fell looks down on its north side.

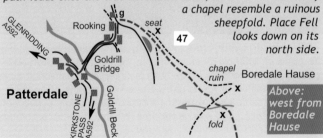

GLENRIDDING A592

Rooking

seat

47

Goldrill Bridge

chapel ruin

Boredale Hause

Patterdale

KIRKSTONE PASS A592

Goldrill Beck

fold

Above: west from Boredale Hause

ANGLE TARN is a lovely sheet of water nestling on a shelf beneath its Pikes. One of two so named in Lakeland, it makes an ideal spot to break up the day's climbing. Its banks have long been a popular location for wild campers, who might savour a beautiful sunset over the Fairfield group to the west. Hopefully you won't experience a sunset at this stage of the day!

Angletarn
Pikes
▲

Dubhow
Beck

48

Celebrity of the fells - a young Herdwick sheep

Angle Tarn, looking west to the Fairfield group

Tamer surrounds crowd in briefly before emergence above the head of Dubhow Beck, a classic moment as Brotherswater appears dramatically far below: this is a mercurial half-hour spell. A choice of higher or lower paths traverse the flank of Angletarn Pikes to the same goal, rounding a corner to find Angle Tarn outspread in front, and the great line of the High Street range marching across the skyline high above.

The path rounds the far side of the tarn and then continues gently on up to a gateway below Satura Crag. Be sure to keep to the right-hand, wallside path at a fork before heading on through the peaty terrain below Rest Dodd. The whole of Hayeswater appears ahead beneath Thornthwaite Crag, and an undulating trek ensues before climbing towards the dome of The Knott (2424ft/739m), merging with a path from Hartsop to reach a wall-corner just beneath the summit.

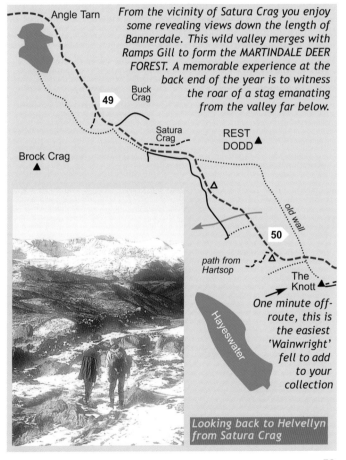

Angle Tarn

From the vicinity of Satura Crag you enjoy some revealing views down the length of Bannerdale. This wild valley merges with Ramps Gill to form the MARTINDALE DEER FOREST. A memorable experience at the back end of the year is to witness the roar of a stag emanating from the valley far below.

49

Buck Crag

Satura Crag

Brock Crag

REST DODD

50

old wall

path from Hartsop

The Knott

One minute off-route, this is the easiest 'Wainwright' fell to add to your collection

Hayeswater

Looking back to Helvellyn from Satura Crag

With the great whaleback of High Street just ahead, the path runs along the wallside to the airy saddle of the Straits of Riggindale. Double back sharply left from this path junction to skirt around the rim of Riggindale to the waiting prow of Kidsty Pike. At 2559ft/780m the summit of the Coast to Coast Walk is very much a place for an extended break, with Haweswater shimmering far below. When it's time to leave, a clear path quickly forms to pass a brace of old shelters on a rash of stones on the declining east ridge. It descends all the way to the lakeshore via the knobbly crest of Kidsty Howes. At the foot of the ridge join the lakeside path, turning left over a bridge on lovely Randale Beck and then along the length of Haweswater. A steep pull to a knoll makes for an alarming early moment.

KIDSTY PIKE has an impressive profile which masks the fact it is merely a minor upthrust on the shoulder of another mountain. Its spectacular drop into Riggindale is no sham, however, nor its position for appraising the craggy eastern face of High Street. Would it be churlish to suggest that the walk's true summit is the marginally higher approach to it, beneath Rampsgill Head?

High Street Roman rd

Rampsgill Head ▲

51

Kidsty Pike ▲

52

Twopenny Crag ✗

Sale Pot

Straits of Riggindale

Sale Pot is a textbook example of a hanging valley left after the last Ice Age

High Street Roman road

↓ summit of High Street

Riggindale Beck

The HIGH STREET ROMAN ROAD is a legendary highway linking the fort at Brougham, near Penrith, with Ambleside. It was their highest way in the country, reaching almost 2700ft/820m on the fell that now bears its name. The bare mountain top saw further action a couple of centuries ago, as a venue for horse races and sports linked with the old Mardale shepherds' meet.

Kidsty Pike from Twopenny Crag

The presence of England's only nesting Golden Eagles on the crags above Riggindale was for many years a major visitor draw, with an RSPB public observation hut just off-route near the foot of Riggindale Beck. Sadly the male lost his partner in 2005, and the chances of attracting another mate look bleak...

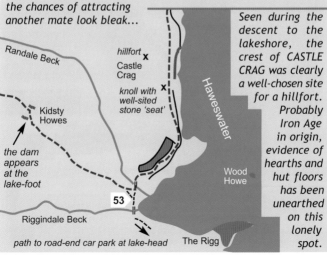

Seen during the descent to the lakeshore, the crest of CASTLE CRAG was clearly a well-chosen site for a hillfort. Probably Iron Age in origin, evidence of hearths and hut floors has been unearthed on this lonely spot.

Randale Beck

hillfort ✗
Castle Crag

knoll with well-sited stone 'seat' ✗

Kidsty Howes

Haweswater

the dam appears at the lake-foot

Wood Howe

53

Riggindale Beck

path to road-end car park at lake-head

The Rigg

A clear path runs the length of Haweswater, always with a wall or fence keeping you from polluting the water. At Measand Beck a short detour upstream reveals lovely waterplay at The Forces. In its later stages the way broadens into a track to drop to a gate, then descends through trees to an access road down to the cottages at Burnbanks, and a junction by the green. If seeking an overnight halt at Bampton or its sister village Bampton Grange (each has a welcoming pub), remain on the road out for an easy half-hour's walk. The main route crosses to a bridle-gate opposite, from where a path runs through delightful woodland onto a road where Naddle Bridge strides over Haweswater Beck.

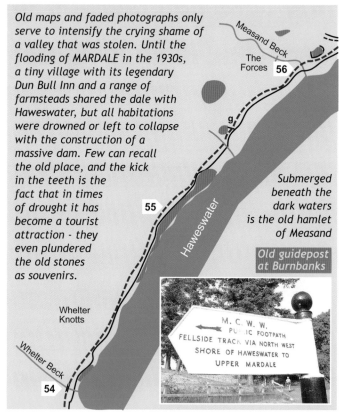

Old maps and faded photographs only serve to intensify the crying shame of a valley that was stolen. Until the flooding of MARDALE in the 1930s, a tiny village with its legendary Dun Bull Inn and a range of farmsteads shared the dale with Haweswater, but all habitations were drowned or left to collapse with the construction of a massive dam. Few can recall the old place, and the kick in the teeth is the fact that in times of drought it has become a tourist attraction - they even plundered the old stones as souvenirs.

Measand Beck

The Forces 56

Haweswater

55

9

Submerged beneath the dark waters is the old hamlet of Measand

Old guidepost at Burnbanks

M. C. W. W.
PUBLIC FOOTPATH
FELLSIDE TRACK VIA NORTH WEST
SHORE OF HAWESWATER TO
UPPER MARDALE

Whelter Knotts

Whelter Beck

54

BURNBANKS is a modest hamlet that began as simple dwellings built for reservoir employees, based around an attractive green with a welcoming seat. Two quaint Manchester Corporation Water Works signposts point the way towards a 'fellside track' - the one you came down.

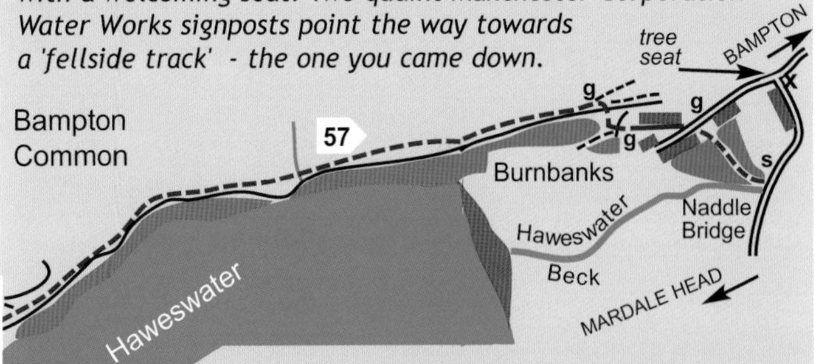

tree seat

BAMPTON

Bampton
Common

57

Burnbanks

Haweswater

Haweswater
Beck

Naddle
Bridge

s

MARDALE HEAD

Beside the path, just before the dam, a plaque records the fact that water from two adjoining side valleys was diverted into Haweswater Reservoir on 3/10/50

*Bluebell woods
at Naddle Bridge*

*On the path at
Haweswater*

6

BURNBANKS TO ORTON

DISTANCE 13¼ miles (21km)   *ASCENT 1215 feet/370m*

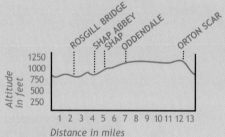

ROSGILL BRIDGE
SHAP ABBEY
SHAP
ODDENDALE
ORTON SCAR

Altitude in feet

1250
1000
750
500
250

1 2 3 4 5 6 7 8 9 10 11 12 13
Distance in miles

A marvellous range of scenery is matched by a remarkable array of features deeply rooted in history during this stage, in which feet can relax having left Lakeland's more challenging fell country behind. The verdant environs of the River Lowther give a lovely approach to Shap Abbey, and beyond its street village the crossing of the Westmorland plateau begins. This is dominated by limestone underfoot and distant views of rolling hills: back to Lakeland, south to the Howgill Fells, and east to the Pennines. The cushioned grasslands of Crosby Ravensworth Fell feature a stone circle amid its antiquities, and you conclude with a delightful stroll down into the warm welcome of Orton. Alternatives are limited, other than north to Crosby Ravensworth or south to Tebay.

Erratic boulder, Crosby Ravensworth Fell

Leave Naddle Bridge by a stile on the east side, immediately crossing the beck by a parallel defunct old pack-bridge, and inflowing Naddle Beck by a footbridge - an interesting corner! Head downstream in the lovely environs of the beck, passing Thornthwaite Force and shapely Park Bridge in quick succession. After a brief break from the beck, a wide track forms to soon rise above a wooded bank to cross a sidestream to a gate/stile. Here forsake the valley of Haweswater Beck by following the fenceside up to the barns of High Park, then steer left across the field to a gate/stile in a hedge. The sketchy path runs a direct course through a couple more fields to the attractive house at Rawhead, following its drive out onto an unfenced road.

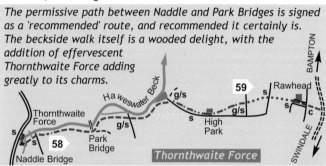

The permissive path between Naddle and Park Bridges is signed as a 'recommended' route, and recommended it certainly is. The beckside walk itself is a wooded delight, with the addition of effervescent Thornthwaite Force adding greatly to its charms.

Cross straight over the road on a path that bears left over gorse-filled moorland to descend to a road at Rosgill Bridge. Barely impinging on the tarmac, however, turn immediately right onto a farm drive heading upstream by the River Lowther. At the right-hand of two gates forsake the drive and keep left with a wall, over a stile and passing below the farm of Good Croft, alongside a fence to discover Parish Crag Bridge on Swindale Beck. Up the bank behind bear left up the field towards a skyline barn, passing through an enclosure occupied by a motley assortment of barns to meet a farm road on a corner.

Turn up the road until the accompanying wall breaks off left, then do likewise by crossing to a stile beyond marshy ground. Follow the wall away to a corner, from where a thin path runs through a large field, short-cutting the wide curve of the wall up to the right. On the brow the tower of Shap Abbey appears, and from a stile at the far corner, one final field is crossed to meet the Lowther again just before the abbey. Curve right above the bank to a stile. Abbey Bridge leads into the abbey car park and onto the road that climbs away, but the abbey ruins can first be inspected by means of the green track just ahead. On leaving, from the farm bridge the hard access road climbs steeply through a field.

Shap Abbey

ROSGILL is a sleepy hamlet of cottages and farms straddling a narrow lane climbing away from the Lowther. If desperate for sustenance, keep on through it to reach Shap more quickly.

The RIVER LOWTHER flows for some sixteen miles from the dam of the Wet Sleddale Reservoir to its entry into the Eamont near Penrith. Its grassy banks are entirely free of man's interference, the only settlement to take advantage being Bampton Grange, which can hardly be regarded as a blemish.

PARISH CRAG BRIDGE is a work of art: this former packhorse bridge nestles in a delectable setting, on a wooded bend of the sizeable watercourse of Swindale Beck

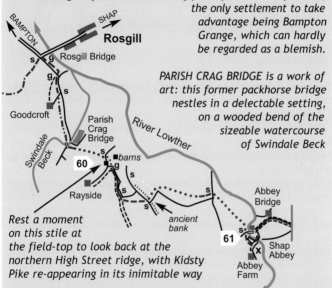

Rest a moment on this stile at the field-top to look back at the northern High Street ridge, with Kidsty Pike re-appearing in its inimitable way

SHAP ABBEY is the only abbey in the old county of Westmorland, and is a rarity also in its proximity to the high mountains. It was founded around the end of the 12th century, and was home to White Canons belonging to the Premonstratensian order (in common with Easby Abbey, some 60 miles further at Richmond). The imposing tower presides over what are otherwise low-lying ruins, much of the stone having found its way into the adjoining farm. Its setting, as ever, is idyllic, and the cost to savour it? Nothing at all. Abbey Bridge has been superseded by a modern structure for the farm's use. Alongside the old bridge is a restored sheepwash. The Lake District National Park is finally vacated here.

At a cattle-grid the road becomes enclosed: you can opt to shun tarmac by taking a stile to the left, and rising parallel through the fields, interrupted by a road before then resuming the course to rejoin the road at the entrance into Shap. Turn right on the main street (A6) for a lengthy stroll through the village.

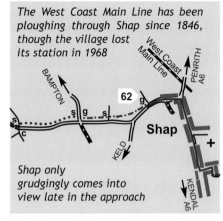

The West Coast Main Line has been ploughing through Shap since 1846, though the village lost its station in 1968

Shap only grudgingly comes into view late in the approach

Leave some time later by Moss Grove on the left opposite the Kings Arms. Quickly turn right on a road that becomes a rough track climbing to bridge the railway. Continuing between hedgerows, bear right at a fork beyond a barn, your green way soon emerging into a field. With the outline of a motorway footbridge ahead, three fields are crossed to earn the satisfaction of crossing the M6, a landmark event. On the other side turn right, and beyond a wall-end the thin path slants up through boulders and hawthorn to a brow, below which is the Hardendale road alongside the isolated house of The Nab. Cross over and bear right on a gentle green way to a wall corner, rising slightly to approach Hardendale Quarry. Follow the wall until a stile on the right leads to a pair of step-flights flanking the quarry road.

SHAP, with its numerous pubs, shops, B&B's, cafe and chippy is a much appreciated staging post of the walk, a role in which it has had much previous experience. Prior to the opening of the M6, the place buzzed with life as the A6 brought all and sundry through, and being the only village on the 25-mile stretch between Kendal and just short of Penrith, it waylaid a good many. South of the village the road attains all but 1400ft/426m, and was notorious for lengthy blockages by snowdrifts. Shap is linear in the extreme, stretching a good mile along either side of the main road with little depth. Centrally placed are the church with some Norman work, and probably the most interesting building, the 300-year old market hall which now houses a heritage centre. In belching evidence are the nearby granite works, and the local Shap granite's pinkish hue adds a sparkle to the many local lanes.

West Coast Main Line

63

Market Hall, Shap

The Nab

HARDENDALE

Hardendale Nab

Hardendale Quarry

M6 MOTORWAY

SHAP

64

lagoons

quarry road

Below............ industry and transport at Shap

On the other side of the quarry road another dusty road heads away towards Oddendale, hidden in trees. Joining its access road turn right, passing the entrance to remain outside its confines on a similarly broad track rising onto grassy moor. Easily missed is Oddendale Stone Circle across to the right, as the broad green way runs on near a plantation to a large, walled pasture. Keeping left of it a slight green way strides on, with Crosby Ravensworth Fell outspread ahead. Continuing on to a slight depression, bear down to the left past a crumbling bield (sheep shelter) to the corner of a plantation, from where a slim path heads up the slope beyond. The grassy course of a Roman road is crossed to rise to a distinct tumulus. Head on through a small limestone pavement to drop to an immense Shap granite boulder. The clear path now descends to cross the embryo River Lyvennet, and with the Black Dub monument off-route a little upstream, the path rises straight ahead to a wall corner.

*Oddendale
Stone Circle*

*The monument
at Black Dub*

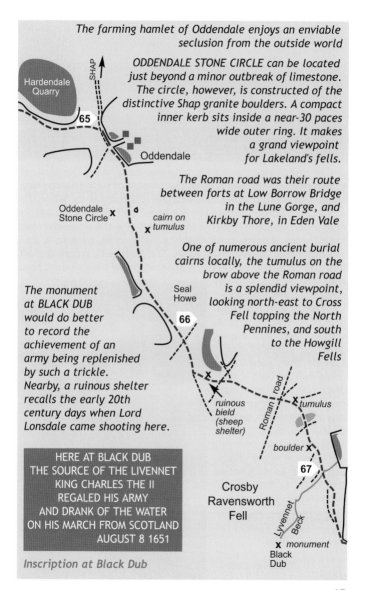

The farming hamlet of Oddendale enjoys an enviable seclusion from the outside world

ODDENDALE STONE CIRCLE can be located just beyond a minor outbreak of limestone. The circle, however, is constructed of the distinctive Shap granite boulders. A compact inner kerb sits inside a near-30 paces wide outer ring. It makes a grand viewpoint for Lakeland's fells.

The Roman road was their route between forts at Low Borrow Bridge in the Lune Gorge, and Kirkby Thore, in Eden Vale

One of numerous ancient burial cairns locally, the tumulus on the brow above the Roman road is a splendid viewpoint, looking north-east to Cross Fell topping the North Pennines, and south to the Howgill Fells

The monument at BLACK DUB would do better to record the achievement of an army being replenished by such a trickle. Nearby, a ruinous shelter recalls the early 20th century days when Lord Lonsdale came shooting here.

Hardendale Quarry

SHAP

65

Oddendale

Oddendale Stone Circle x

cairn on
x tumulus

Seal Howe

66

ruinous bield (sheep shelter)

Roman road

x tumulus

boulder x

67

HERE AT BLACK DUB
THE SOURCE OF THE LIVENNET
KING CHARLES THE II
REGALED HIS ARMY
AND DRANK OF THE WATER
ON HIS MARCH FROM SCOTLAND
AUGUST 8 1651

Inscription at Black Dub

Crosby Ravensworth Fell

Livennet Beck

x monument
Black Dub

At the corner the wall is followed away along the heather moor-edge, descending around the outside of park-like country, rising past Robin Hood's Grave and then climbing away. When the wall parts company head over the brow, and with an old quarry as a target, descend to a stile in a fence lining the moorland road from Crosby Ravensworth. Slanting right, cross over to a trod heading for a slender plantation. The thin path traces its left side and continues gently up to the meeting of the previous road with the B6260 Appleby road, a superb moment.

Crossing the cattle-grid drop left to a gate, and a green way curves down to Broadfell Farm. Across the yard slant down to the field corner below. A path runs by a tiny stream, crossing it to run a delightful parallel course, becoming fully enclosed before emerging into a corner of the village. Bear right to a junction and right to the B6260, then left for the centre.

Above: Dusk on Orton Scar, looking back to Kidsty Pike

Right: in Orton

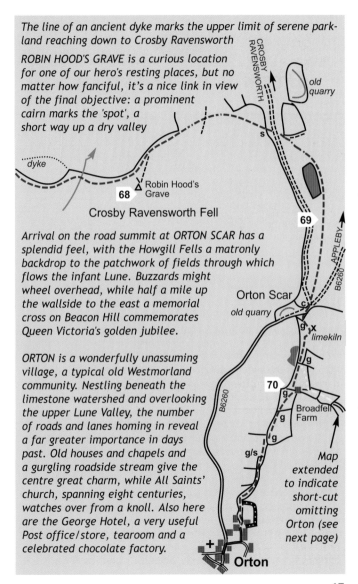

The line of an ancient dyke marks the upper limit of serene parkland reaching down to Crosby Ravensworth

ROBIN HOOD'S GRAVE is a curious location for one of our hero's resting places, but no matter how fanciful, it's a nice link in view of the final objective: a prominent cairn marks the 'spot', a short way up a dry valley

CROSBY RAVENSWORTH

old quarry

s

dyke

△ Robin Hood's
68   Grave

Crosby Ravensworth Fell

69

APPLEBY

B6260

Arrival on the road summit at ORTON SCAR has a splendid feel, with the Howgill Fells a matronly backdrop to the patchwork of fields through which flows the infant Lune. Buzzards might wheel overhead, while half a mile up the wallside to the east a memorial cross on Beacon Hill commemorates Queen Victoria's golden jubilee.

Orton Scar

old quarry

c

g x
limekiln

g

ORTON is a wonderfully unassuming village, a typical old Westmorland community. Nestling beneath the limestone watershed and overlooking the upper Lune Valley, the number of roads and lanes homing in reveal a far greater importance in days past. Old houses and chapels and a gurgling roadside stream give the centre great charm, while All Saints' church, spanning eight centuries, watches over from a knoll. Also here are the George Hotel, a very useful Post office/store, tearoom and a celebrated chocolate factory.

70

g

Broadfell
Farm

g

g

B6260

g/s

Map
extended
to indicate
short-cut
omitting
Orton (see
next page)

✝
Orton

7

ORTON TO KIRKBY STEPHEN

DISTANCE 12³4 miles (20¹2km)   *ASCENT 1100 feet/335m*

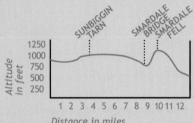

The splendid scenery of this stage is enjoyed during some very easy walking across Ravenstonedale Moor, Crosby Garrett Fell and Smardale Fell. The Westmorland plateau again features lush limestone terrain and continuing views, more notably the nearer Howgills and the fast-approaching Pennines. Particularly memorable landmarks that form integral parts of this grand march are the extensive upland pool of Sunbiggin Tarn and the deep cleft of secretive Smardale. A further, greater concentration of features of antiquity include another stone circle, prehistoric settlements and burial chambers. Your day finishes on the banks of the River Eden, at the foot of the Pennines.

There are a number of alternative routes, either southerly through the upper Lune Valley through farming hamlets along the base of the Howgill Fells (or even over them, if feeling energetic) to Newbiggin-on-Lune and Ravenstonedale; or northerly to Great Asby Scar, Little Asby, Potts Valley and Crosby Garrett.

The original course of the Coast to Coast Walk has been diverted from some sensitive wildlife habitats and archaeological sites where its route was neither public nor permissive: the route described in the following pages includes both previously ignored and newly created rights of way, and also a permissive path.

Leave Orton by crossing the main road from the square, over a tiny green and footbridge from where an urban path runs past playing fields to another stream and a back road. A snicket between houses opposite sends the way along a fieldside to join a narrow back lane. A few paces right another stile sends the largely invisible path off through several fields, ultimately slanting right to a stile onto the Raisbeck road. Go briefly left to a farm drive on the left just past a house, then slant diagonally off it to a stile in the far corner. This empties onto the unsurfaced Knott Lane: look over the wall opposite to view Gamelands Stone Circle. Just a few yards to the left, take a stile on the right to commence another field section through further innumerable stiles, the first being in a kink of a wall ahead.

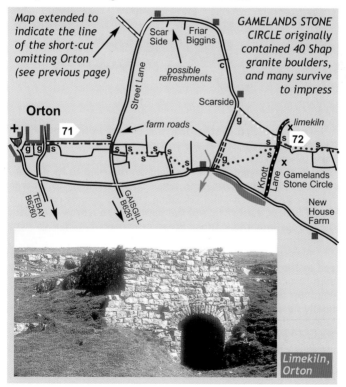

Map extended to indicate the line of the short-cut omitting Orton (see previous page)

Scar Side

Friar Biggins

GAMELANDS STONE CIRCLE originally contained 40 Shap granite boulders, and many survive to impress

Street Lane

possible refreshments

c

Scarside

Orton

farm roads

g

limekiln

71

s

s   s   s

s   s

s

72

s

s

g

Knott Lane

Gamelands Stone Circle

TEBAY B6260

GAISGILL B6261

New House Farm

Limekiln, Orton

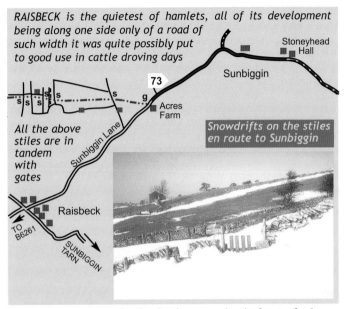

RAISBECK is the quietest of hamlets, all of its development being along one side only of a road of such width it was quite possibly put to good use in cattle droving days

Stoneyhead Hall

Sunbiggin

73

Acres Farm

All the above stiles are in tandem with gates

Sunbiggin Lane

Raisbeck

TO B6261

SUNBIGGIN TARN

Snowdrifts on the stiles en route to Sunbiggin

The succession of stiles lead on, passing in front of a barn. Two final, larger pastures are crossed to emerge onto Sunbiggin Lane by the large house at Acres Farm. Turn left to the farming hamlet of Sunbiggin, and keep right on the road to its demise, where a pleasant green lane takes up the running to emerge onto heathery Tarn Moor. Heading away to a crossroads in a grassy hollow, turn right and the path rises to a brow. The path then drops to another broad green crossroads in a dip: go right to emerge onto the open road above hidden Sunbiggin Tarn.

Turn right, dropping gently to a modest bridge on Tarn Sike, and as the road starts rising just beyond, go left on an inviting path through the heather. With a marshy basin down to the left you soon reach a path crossroads: go left, pleasantly on again to finally reveal a good prospect of the tarn backed by limestone heights. The broadening way drops to a gate in a boundary wall. Trading heather moor for grassy moor the green way resumes, crossing a boardwalk on a marsh and rising gently away across open grassy surrounds. It continues over a gentle brow and down to a dip, up and on again to drop steadily past an island pasture.

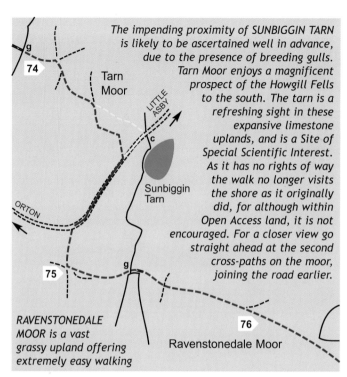

The impending proximity of SUNBIGGIN TARN is likely to be ascertained well in advance, due to the presence of breeding gulls. Tarn Moor enjoys a magnificent prospect of the Howgill Fells to the south. The tarn is a refreshing sight in these expansive limestone uplands, and is a Site of Special Scientific Interest. As it has no rights of way the walk no longer visits the shore as it originally did, for although within Open Access land, it is not encouraged. For a closer view go straight ahead at the second cross-paths on the moor, joining the road earlier.

74

g

Tarn Moor

LITTLE ASBY

c

Sunbiggin Tarn

ORTON

75

g

76

RAVENSTONEDALE MOOR is a vast grassy upland offering extremely easy walking

Ravenstonedale Moor

Sunbiggin Tarn

At Severals

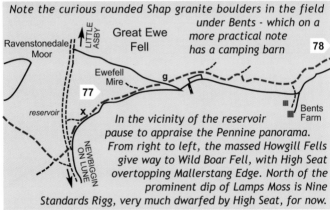

Note the curious rounded Shap granite boulders in the field under Bents - which on a more practical note has a camping barn

78

Ravenstonedale Moor

LITTLE ASBY

Great Ewe Fell

Ewefell Mire

g

77

reservoir

x

Bents Farm

NEWBIGGIN ON LUNE

In the vicinity of the reservoir pause to appraise the Pennine panorama. From right to left, the massed Howgill Fells give way to Wild Boar Fell, with High Seat overtopping Mallerstang Edge. North of the prominent dip of Lamps Moss is Nine Standards Rigg, very much dwarfed by High Seat, for now.

As the path approaches a moorland road it meets a stony access road: turn left up this the short way to the road at a wall corner, and follow an initially sketchy wallside way rising gently left to meet a track. Turning right this quickly ends at a covered reservoir: keep on with the wall along the tapering pasture to a gate at the end. The green way continues along the wallside beyond nearby Bents to the next gate in the wall. From it follow a wall away to a stile, and remain with the wall as it rises to the brow. A lovely path descends towards Smardale with Severals settlement just to the right. Swing right on approaching derelict cottages to reach a bridge over a former railway. Go right a short way to descend to waiting Smardale Bridge. Across it a superb old way breasts the steep slope, which soon relents to enjoy a gentle traverse of the wide open spaces of Smardale Fell.

The expanse of Crosby Garrett Fell is an archaeologists' paradise, and the largest of its prehistoric field systems is the SEVERALS village settlement, where a labyrinth of grassy mounds formed hut enclosures amid converging field boundaries

Crosby Garrett Fell

As well as the impressive viaduct, look for the 'on-site' quarry - with imposing double kiln - in this fascinating side-valley of SMARDALE. A nature reserve and walking trails now exist here.

g

s

earthwork on brow

x

ex-railway cottages

former railway

Scandal Beck

Smardalegill Viaduct

(on former Darlington-Tebay line)

Severals

79

Giants' Graves

80

fold

g

On the brow above Severals, pause to survey the superb prospect of Smardale, with the walk scaling the hillside opposite

g

Smardale Bridge

g

Intriguingly named GIANTS' GRAVES are shown more descriptively on maps as 'pillow mounds': of uncertain origin, it is possible they were constructed as rabbit warrens some time since introduction into Britain by the Normans

Paths at either end of Smardale Bridge lead through a 16th century deer park to the lovely village of Ravenstonedale

Old kiln, Smardale

The *SETTLE-CARLISLE RAILWAY* is probably the most famous line in the country, thanks in part to the monumental campaign that culminated in its salvation in 1989. It was completed in 1876 after seven hard years when Victorian endeavour reached new heights to battle against the Pennine terrain and associated weather, and was the work of the Midland Railway who were determined to create their own main line through to Scotland. With more sensible routes to east and west, they resorted to the stern challenge of the high Pennines. Logical approaches via Ribblesdale and the Eden Valley led to the central massif from Ribblehead to Mallerstang, where spectacular engineering feats created deep tunnels alternating with tall viaducts.

The Settle-Carlisle story now moves on a full century to witness efforts to close the line which ultimately proved keener than those to open it.... The railway killers were not prepared for an equally determined defence of the line by an outraged public: a reasoned, eloquently-argued case for its retention, based on common sense and hard facts - not merely nostalgia - was so strong that it is now difficult to imagine that back in 1989 closure was so dangerously near. As you encounter the line it has just broken free of the enveloping Pennines and is set for an extended, triumphal journey through the Eden Valley.

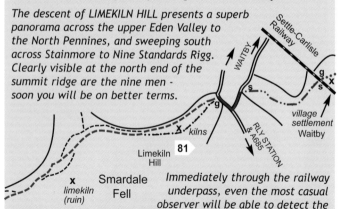

The descent of *LIMEKILN HILL* presents a superb panorama across the upper Eden Valley to the North Pennines, and sweeping south across Stainmore to Nine Standards Rigg. Clearly visible at the north end of the summit ridge are the nine men - soon you will be on better terms.

Immediately through the railway underpass, even the most casual observer will be able to detect the *WAITBY* village settlement. Just to the right are distinct outlines of a rectangular earthwork with an arrangement of internal enclosures, not all destroyed by the railway embankment.

Looking back over Smardale

At GREEN RIGGS the defunct railway line from Darlington was preparing to divide, a branch going north to meet the Settle-Carlisle line at Appleby, the other heading west to the main line at Tebay - what journeys were once possible! A little south of the farm was Kirkby Stephen East, still west of the town but not as much as the 'West' station, which remains, on the Settle-Carlisle line. Long-term plans may eventually see the old line through the East station operating again.

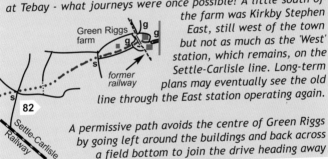

A permissive path avoids the centre of Green Riggs by going left around the buildings and back across a field bottom to join the drive heading away

Rising gently to a brow on Smardale Fell the nearby wall drops away: avoid any branches going that way and keep on to find another wall quickly returning. Variant paths descend near it, either side of two limekilns to a gate onto a narrow road. Follow it right just as far as a junction, then go left to a stile on the right. A thin way winds round a large field to a railway underpass ahead. From it bear gently right to locate a stile by a wall corner. Just into the field is the long-awaited first glimpse of Kirkby Stephen. Slanting down a small field the head of a dry hollow is rounded as the way slants left, down through a large pasture to a wall-stile at the bottom by a few trees. Descend past an island barn to a defunct double railway underpass to enter the yard of Green Riggs Farm.

75

Kirkby Stephen

At Green Riggs the way passes through two gates on the right and then out along the farm road all the way to Kirkby, passing the flat-topped Croglam Castle site up to the right. The back lane - not a classic entry to the town - can be followed as far as desired, though the main road can be joined much earlier. An option is to keep on as far as the rear of the Pennine Hotel, just past which an alleyway leads into the centre opposite the Market Place - the point at which it will be left tomorrow.

CROGLAM CASTLE is thought to have been the location of an Iron Age Brigante tribe's hillfort. A ditch and rampart are left, and a stile beneath it may tempt a brief investigation.

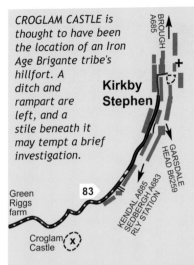

KIRKBY STEPHEN is small, tiny even as towns go, but in the heart of a vast rural area its importance is far greater. Its market charter was granted in 1361, and today the Market Place remains at the heart of things. Various characterful buildings are grouped around, with the church of St Stephen, dating in parts from the mid-13th century, framed neatly behind the Cloisters of 1810. Inside, the Wharton and Musgrave chapels have effigies of members of these once influential local families.

Pride of place goes to the Loki Stone, part of a 1000 year old Norse cross featuring a bound devil: Loki was a Viking god, and the carving is thought to symbolise Christianity overcoming paganism. Alongside the church is the old parsonage dating from 1677, and also the old Grammar School, founded by Lord Thomas Wharton of Wharton Hall in 1566 and in use as such for almost 400 years. Across the main road is an old knitting gallery in what is known as the Shambles.

There is a gaunt Temperance Hall of 1856, while the Methodist chapel of 1889 now serves as a fine youth hostel. Its predecessor was across the street above the Friends' Meeting House, an unfashionable but homely place: in use from 1931 it was one of the very first in the country. Like Shap before it, Kirkby Stephen clings to its main road and displays little width. An old roadsign still indicates distances in miles and furlongs (a measurement retained in the world of horse-racing), and an excellent information centre operates. Another useful feature is a welcoming number of cafes to complement the handful of pubs and range of shops. Also here is an outdoor shop, a bookshop, banks, chemist and several chippies! In 2010 a small brewery was established.

8

KIRKBY STEPHEN TO KELD

DISTANCE *12 miles (19km)*   **ASCENT** *1900 feet/580m*

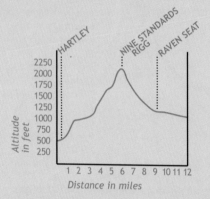

This is the crossing of the Pennine watershed, the backbone of England. Nine Standards Rigg is also a very suitable place to celebrate such an occasion, being an outstanding viewpoint and endowed with a famous family of beacons. Its ascent is remarkably easy, for the most part on grass verges or green trackways: only the upper limits remind you that a mountain has been climbed. The long descent to the headwaters of the Swale is true Pennine in character, a wild country that changes little on arrival in Whitsundale: only on nearing Keld is there a warmer feel.

As the route over Nine Standards was never a right of way (though has since fallen into Open Access land), the authorities negotiated colour-coded permissive routes based on seasons of the year, partly to allow the ground to recover from erosion. The two main routes diverge after leaving the summit, clearly identified in the text and on the maps. A third, safer option recommended in the first edition of this guide has been taken up as the 'official' line in poor weather or in winter, and this too is clearly described. All variants re-unite before reaching Raven Seat.

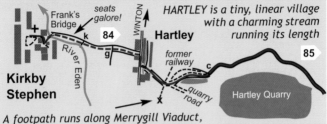

Frank's Bridge · seats galore! · WINTON · 84 · k · g · River Eden · Kirkby Stephen

HARTLEY is a tiny, linear village with a charming stream running its length

Hartley · former railway · c · 85 · quarry road · x · Hartley Quarry

A footpath runs along Merrygill Viaduct, just a minute off-route on this section of the old Stainmore line

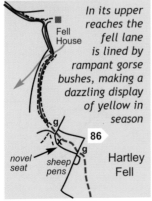

The Eden, Frank's Bridge

In its upper reaches the fell lane is lined by rampant gorse bushes, making a dazzling display of yellow in season

Fell House · g · 86 · novel seat · sheep pens · g · Hartley Fell

Leave the Market Place outside the church by the short lane past the WCs, descending Stoneshot and cutting down a snicket to cross the River Eden at Frank's Bridge. Turn right with the river just as far as a bend, and from the kissing-gate take a surfaced wallside path away from the river. It runs on to join a back road in sleepy Hartley. Go briefly right, taking a path down to a slab footbridge. Continue right on a parallel road behind, which quickly swings left to climb past the entrance to Hartley Quarry. Sanity returns as the lane eventually levels out to approach isolated Fell House. It runs on still further to end at a fork, where the left branch rises through a gate onto Hartley Fell.

79

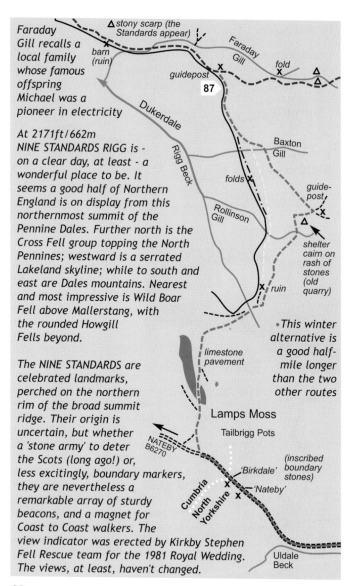

Faraday Gill recalls a local family whose famous offspring Michael was a pioneer in electricity

stony scarp (the Standards appear)

Faraday Gill

barn (ruin)

fold

guidepost

87

Dukerdale

Rigg Beck

Baxton Gill

folds

guide-post

Rollinson Gill

shelter cairn on rash of stones (old quarry)

ruin

At 2171ft/662m NINE STANDARDS RIGG is - on a clear day, at least - a wonderful place to be. It seems a good half of Northern England is on display from this northernmost summit of the Pennine Dales. Further north is the Cross Fell group topping the North Pennines; westward is a serrated Lakeland skyline; while to south and east are Dales mountains. Nearest and most impressive is Wild Boar Fell above Mallerstang, with the rounded Howgill Fells beyond.

The NINE STANDARDS are celebrated landmarks, perched on the northern rim of the broad summit ridge. Their origin is uncertain, but whether a 'stone army' to deter the Scots (long ago!) or, less excitingly, boundary markers, they are nevertheless a remarkable array of sturdy beacons, and a magnet for Coast to Coast walkers. The view indicator was erected by Kirkby Stephen Fell Rescue team for the 1981 Royal Wedding. The views, at least, haven't changed.

• This winter alternative is a good half-mile longer than the two other routes

limestone pavement

Lamps Moss

Tailbrigg Pots

NATEBY B6270

(inscribed boundary stones)

'Birkdale'

'Nateby'

Cumbria

North Yorkshire

Uldale Beck

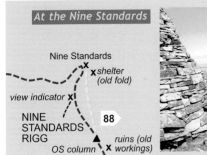

At the Nine Standards

Nine Standards

X shelter (old fold)

view indicator **X**

NINE STANDARDS RIGG

88

▲ ruins (old workings)

OS column **X**

With the Nine Standards seen intermittently ahead, the broad track soon rises by a wall. As the going eases, wall and track slant right, and at a guidepost the route leaves the public bridleway. Here departs the first seasonal variation.

DECEMBER-APRIL Remain on the delectable wallside way, rising a little further before a level, grassy march. A little further it leaves the wall to rise gently over the fell. Beyond Baxton Gill it is a thinner path slanting up through reeds, then more gently on to a junction. From this high point turn sharp right, descending 100 yards to a ruinous shelter cairn above a rash of stones. A path drops away, swinging left as a splendid made way down to cross a stream and on towards the wall enclosing the head of Dukerdale. From the wall corner drop to cross the stream, but up the other side bear left as the wall turns right. A gentle green way runs above a tiny pool to approach a limestone pavement: around its start keep right on a more inviting green way, rising gently through part of the pavement and at the other end meeting a broader grass track. Go left on this, and reaching a fork, keep left to meet the summit of the B6270. Ahead is rounded High Pike Hill. Go left past myriad boundary signs as the road angles down for a long descent into the headwaters of the Swale.

MAY-NOVEMBER The guidepost sends a similarly distinct green track directly up the fell. This soon resumes shadowing Faraday Gill, rising above a ravine to a brace of cairns framing the impending Standards. Bridging a small marsh behind, the 'built' path rises over less comfortable terrain amongst peat groughs before gaining the beacons. Visible to the south is the Ordnance Survey column on the summit of the fell, and the main path runs easily thereto, taking in a prominent view indicator en route.

MAY-NOVEMBER The walk continues south past old workings, down to a peaty saddle before White Mossy Hill. Across these groughs a guidepost heralds the second seasonal variation.

AUGUST-NOVEMBER A path turns sharp left down a broad swathe of glutinous peat, descending ever gently towards the side valley of Whitsundale. Marker posts highlight the moist route.

MAY-JULY Keep straight on and up a minor rise to White Mossy Hill, marked by a couple of recumbent stones. The path continues a gradual, peaty descent towards Swaledale. Beyond a shelter cairn on a rash of stones, a prominent 8ft pillar on the far more substantial rocks of Millstones makes an obvious halting place. At the end of the rocks ignore a grass track right (it rapidly becomes a stony track): instead keep to the less obvious path bearing left (odd marker posts). Crossing a simple footbridge at the head of well-defined Mould Gill, it soon swings right to move increasingly pleasantly down to meet a shooters' track. Its hard surface is followed left only as far as the cabin it serves.

DECEMBER-APRIL The road is followed for a mile and a half through bleak, rolling moorland, initially gently declining then remaining largely level. Leave just past a bend when a guidepost sends an invisible path left: a minute further a firm shooters' track (the second passed) leaves the road. Go left on this, initially climbing before running on to its demise above a shooting cabin.

The pillar on Millstones

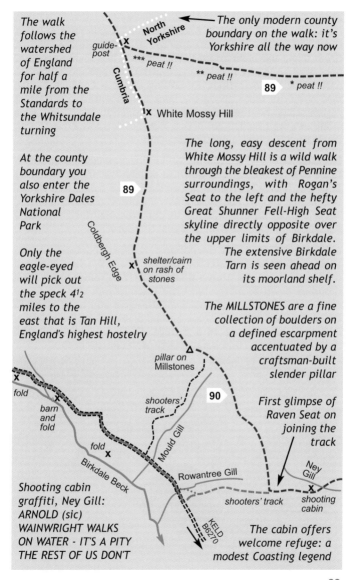

The walk follows the watershed of England for half a mile from the Standards to the Whitsundale turning

The only modern county boundary on the walk: it's Yorkshire all the way now

guidepost

North Yorkshire

Cumbria

*** peat !!

** peat !!

89 * peat !!

X White Mossy Hill

At the county boundary you also enter the Yorkshire Dales National Park

89

Coldbergh Edge

Only the eagle-eyed will pick out the speck 4½ miles to the east that is Tan Hill, England's highest hostelry

The long, easy descent from White Mossy Hill is a wild walk through the bleakest of Pennine surroundings, with Rogan's Seat to the left and the hefty Great Shunner Fell-High Seat skyline directly opposite over the upper limits of Birkdale. The extensive Birkdale Tarn is seen ahead on its moorland shelf.

X shelter/cairn on rash of stones

The MILLSTONES are a fine collection of boulders on a defined escarpment accentuated by a craftsman-built slender pillar

pillar on Millstones

shooters' track

90

Mould Gill

First glimpse of Raven Seat on joining the track

X fold

X barn and fold

fold X

Birkdale Beck

Rowantree Gill

Ney Gill

X shooting cabin

Shooting cabin graffiti, Ney Gill: ARNOLD (sic) WAINWRIGHT WALKS ON WATER - IT'S A PITY THE REST OF US DON'T

shooters' track

KELD B6270

The cabin offers welcome refuge: a modest Coasting legend

AUGUST-NOVEMBER Just short of the valley floor the path drops right towards Whitsundale Beck, and runs a generally pleasant course down this once unfrequented dale. Beyond the folds at Great Cogill the older route takes a higher, less inviting course, now superseded by a drier, more attractive and more obvious path along the dale floor. Re-uniting at Little Cogill, the path now does rise more above the beck before entering a tract of regenerating heather moorland. It descends again and runs along to a wall, which deflects it right, over a low brow to join the main RED route alongside Ney Gill.

DECEMBER-JULY From the hut a more accommodating footpath takes over to drop gently down to engage the company of Ney Gill. This is briefly crossed at two successive points as a fence/wall nudge you off course: a grassy shooters' track forms here, while a small path avoids the second crossing. Just beyond, a guidepost indicates arrival of the BLUE route.

ALL 3 RE-UNITED Noting the option of the firm shooters' track to your right head downstream, quickly crossing when the wall does and rising with it on a thinner path to a minor brow, then dropping down to merge with the track to join the cul-de-sac road into Raven Seat. Cross the cattle-grid and head along to enter the hamlet over a stone-arched bridge. Turn immediately right over another, up to a cottage. From a gate/stile on the right head downstream parallel with Whitsundale Beck.

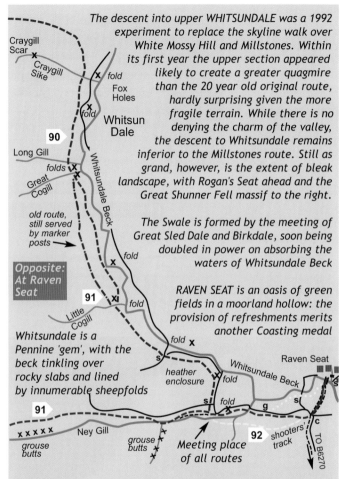

The descent into upper WHITSUNDALE was a 1992 experiment to replace the skyline walk over White Mossy Hill and Millstones. Within its first year the upper section appeared likely to create a greater quagmire than the 20 year old original route, hardly surprising given the more fragile terrain. While there is no denying the charm of the valley, the descent to Whitsundale remains inferior to the Millstones route. Still as grand, however, is the extent of bleak landscape, with Rogan's Seat ahead and the Great Shunner Fell massif to the right.

The Swale is formed by the meeting of Great Sled Dale and Birkdale, soon being doubled in power on absorbing the waters of Whitsundale Beck

RAVEN SEAT is an oasis of green fields in a moorland hollow: the provision of refreshments merits another Coasting medal

Whitsundale is a Pennine 'gem', with the beck tinkling over rocky slabs and lined by innumerable sheepfolds

Craygill Scar x
Craygill Sike
x fold
Fox Holes
x fold
Whitsun Dale
90
Long Gill
folds x
Great Cogill
x x
Whitsundale Beck
old route, still served by marker posts →
Opposite: At Raven Seat
x fold
91
x x fold
Little Cogill
fold x
s
heather enclosure
x fold
Whitsundale Beck
Raven Seat
s
s fold
91
x x x x x
Ney Gill
grouse butts
grouse butts x x
Meeting place of all routes
92
shooters' track
g
s
c
TO B6270

In the final section to the Raven Seat road, a small gate on the brow on the left (see map) indicates a variation approach to the farm, which slants right down to a ladder-stile by the beck and then follows it around to the bridge at the road-end. This is in fact the true right of way, though it has largely been usurped by the path remaining on the moor to the cattle-grid.

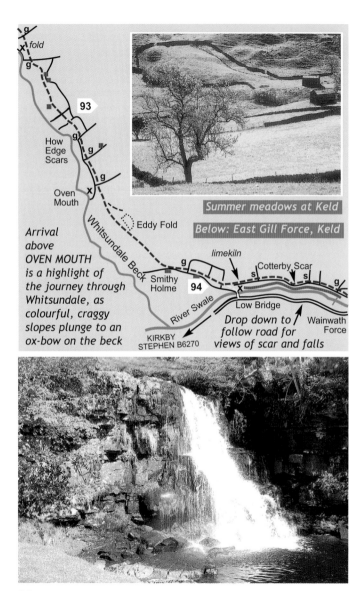

g

x fold

g

93

How
Edge
Scars

g

g

g

Oven
Mouth

x

Whitsundale Beck

Eddy Fold

Summer meadows at Keld

Below: East Gill Force, Keld

*Arrival
above
OVEN MOUTH
is a highlight of
the journey through
Whitsundale, as
colourful, craggy
slopes plunge to an
ox-bow on the beck*

limekiln

g

Cotterby Scar

Smithy
Holme

94

s

s

g

x

Low Bridge

River Swale

*Drop down to
follow road for
views of scar and falls*

Wainwath
Force

KIRKBY
STEPHEN B6270

86

From a gate just beyond, a broad green path climbs left to a barn, then on a level course past further barns and gateways amid rough pastures. After gazing into the splendid wooded gorge of How Edge Scars, several level pastures with a wall for company precede emergence through a last gate into a dramatic scene above Oven Mouth. Advancing across open country the path soon forks: take the right one to pass along the bottom side of a large crumbling enclosure, Eddy Fold. With intermittent moist sections a guidepost beyond it points the way down to the barns of Smithy Holme ahead. Follow their access track left to a corner gate to drop past another abandoned farm.

Just a little further, before the track drops to stone-arched Low Bridge, a thin path bears left above an old wall to begin a level stroll above the full length of the top of Cotterby Scar. Though a grand path, it offers only glimpses of the scar itself: bluebells take advantage of the shelter of the trees atop the scar. From a gate at the end the way shadows an old wall across open pasture: Wainwath Force below is largely obscured by trees. At a thinner right fork slant down to a corner stile onto the road to join the B6270, crossing Park Bridge where you earn a better view of Wainwath Force just upstream. Turn left at the junction for a steady stroll along the road into Keld.

KELD is the first outpost of any size in Swaledale, most of this Norse settlement being set around a tiny square just below the main road: refreshments are usually available at Park Lodge. Just along from it a chapel of 1861 boasts a fine old sundial: alongside are WCs. A Great War memorial remembers four men who never returned to their farming hamlet. The fact that this delectable spot marks the junction of Pennine Way and Coast to Coast Walk was insufficient to save its youth hostel from closure: today the former shooting lodge of Keld Lodge may be a more expensive replacement, but its welcome presence has brought licensed premises back to Keld for the first time since the closure of the Cat Hole Inn in the 1950s. And by the way, you're halfway!

TAN HILL

Currack Force

Park Bridge

River Swale

Catrake Force

95

Keld

Keld Lodge

MUKER B6270

9

KELD TO REETH

DISTANCE 11 miles (17½km)   **ASCENT** 1650 feet/500m

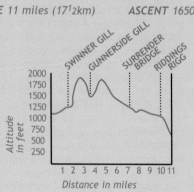

This direct march over the moors is short but time-consuming, certainly if taking interest in the wealth of remains of a once-thriving lead industry. In the recesses of Swinner Gill, Gunnerside Gill and Hard Level Gill are the ruins of smelt mills and associated workings, while the intervening moortops still sport vast tracts of mining debris. It's not all savage industrial wilderness however, for charming deep-cut gills and purple heather moors are inter-spersed, and in the latter stages the mining scenes give way entirely to the softer surrounds of Swaledale at its brilliant best.

The only unfortunate aspect of this route is that it does not more satisfyingly combine moorland and valley scenery, and for this reason many choose to take the valley option, which more than does justice to the beautiful rushing Swale. This runs an entirely different, parallel course shadowing the river down-stream. Riverside paths ensure the Swale's north bank is rarely forsaken, and the innumerable stiles fail to compensate for the ups and downs of the moors route. Last but not least, this enticing alternative has one (or rather several) further advantages, namely a variety of refreshment venues throughout its length.

Leave the bottom right corner of the square by a broad, walled path past a barn. Quickly reaching a fork, take the left branch dropping steeply to a footbridge on the Swale. Across, a path curves up above East Gill Force to a famous junction where the Pennine Way turns off left. Turn right over the stone-arched bridge and a broad track rises away, up through a gate and on above a steep, fenced scree slope high above the gorge. At the end it opens out to swing round past a barn beneath lead mining remains to a fork. Remain on the higher left branch, which quickly runs on above Crackpot Hall. The track slants up and along as a grassy way to a gate to enter the confines of Swinner Gill. The path slants in across a heather flank to a stone-arched bridge beneath the ravine of Swinnergill Kirk: en route note a fine waterfall at the foot of the side valley of East Grain. The path now heads up this past the remains of a lead smelting mill.

The setting of East Gill Force is Arcadian, and a well-chosen spot to share with Pennine Wayfarers leaving Swaledale's loveliness for Tan Hill's wilderness

East Stonesdale

East Gill

East Gill Force

Swinner Gill is a hugely colourful ravine

Beldi Hill

Swinnergill Lead Mines

smelt mill

97

X

g   g   **96**

falls

Keld

MUKER B6270

Kisdon Force

Crackpot Hall

River Swale

x

g

Swinner Gill

Crackpot Hall is a farm abandoned due to mining subsidence

East Grain, Swinner Gill

As the gradient eases, marshy ground and an old fold are encountered just before joining a stony shooters' track. This rises left before running along the moortop to a junction on the very brow, just beyond a gate. Keep straight on to soon overlook the valley of Gunnerside Gill. Beyond a fold, as the track swings right, cairns signal the departure of your path off to the left through heather. It first runs along the upper reach of North Hush's ravine, then slants down to contour above Blakethwaite Smelt Mill before a zigzag down to reach it.

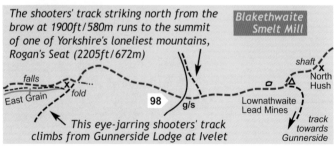

The shooters' track striking north from the brow at 1900ft/580m runs to the summit of one of Yorkshire's loneliest mountains, Rogan's Seat (2205ft/672m)

Blakethwaite Smelt Mill

falls
East Grain
fold

shaft
North Hush

98 g/s

Lownathwaite Lead Mines

track towards Gunnerside

This eye-jarring shooters' track climbs from Gunnerside Lodge at Ivelet

Cross the slab bridge and take a short zigzag path directly behind the ruin to climb to a broad green way. Turn right along this lovely terraced path, with views down the gill's wooded lower reaches. Advance a short way until a small cairn signals a thinner path doubling back left up beneath a small scree slope, leaving that behind and slanting gently up through heather. At a cairn it bears more up to the right, thin but clear as it doubles gently back to slant right (broader now) up through splendid heather terrain to suddenly emerge onto a hard, level former miners' track. Turn right on this for a long, high-level stride through a scene of untold devastation at the Old Gang Mines.

BLAKETHWAITE SMELT MILL was built around 1820, and its best surviving feature is the peat store, whose ruinous form might be equally at home at Shap or Mount Grace. A semi-circular kiln sits high on the bank behind, where the old flue rose up the steep bank. Amidst the ruins a large slab takes you over the beck. Further exploration might include a short detour up the west bank for a closer look at Blakethwaite Force (visible from the bridge). Enthusiasts can continue still further up the gill to the Blakethwaite lead mines and dams before returning.

Blakethwaite
Smelt Mill

Blakethwaite
Force

Blind
Gill

99

Friarfold Moor

stone shelters
X

X

Merry Field

100

Old Gang
Lead Mines

Gunnerside Gill

Gunnerside Beck

X
Bunton
Crushing
Mill

Melbecks Moor

The lead mines and ancillary workings are as much a part of Swaledale as the waterfalls of Keld, and this side-valley of GUNNERSIDE GILL is an excellent venue for their inspection. Indeed, this is arguably the grandest small valley in the whole of the Dales. On the descent to and climb from the gill, the main eye-catching features are the hushes, created by the release of previously dammed-up water which tore away the hillside in the search for workable veins.

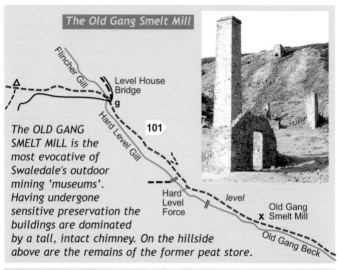

The Old Gang Smelt Mill

Flincher Gill

Level House Bridge

g

Hard Level Gill

101

Hard Level Force

level

Old Gang Smelt Mill **x**

Old Gang Beck

The OLD GANG SMELT MILL is the most evocative of Swaledale's outdoor mining 'museums'. Having undergone sensitive preservation the buildings are dominated by a tall, intact chimney. On the hillside above are the remains of the former peat store.

The track gradually drops to meet Hard Level Gill at stone-arched Level House Bridge, where another track merges from the left. As Hard Level Gill it leads your track down past more recent small-scale barytes extraction workings and Hard Level Force in a colourful ravine to the Old Gang Smelt Mill, seen well in advance. Before reaching it you encounter an arched level by the track and a stone-arched bridge on the beck. Remain on the track (the beck is now known as Old Gang Beck) for a further mile to join a moorland road above Surrender Bridge. Cross straight over the road and away along a clear path, passing above Surrender Smelt Mill and on through heather to negotiate a crossing of steep-walled Cringley Bottom. A stile in the wall at the other side precedes a much steadier jaunt on a broadening way, with the profile of Calver Hill directly in front.

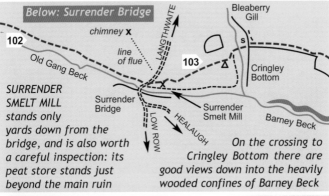

Below: Surrender Bridge

102

chimney **x**

line
of flue

LANGTHWAITE

Bleaberry
Gill

s

103

Cringley
Bottom

Old Gang Beck

SURRENDER
SMELT MILL
*stands only
yards down from the
bridge, and is also worth
a careful inspection: its
peat store stands just
beyond the main ruin*

Surrender
Bridge

LOW ROW

HEALAUGH

Surrender
Smelt Mill

Barney Beck

*On the crossing to
Cringley Bottom there are
good views down into the heavily
wooded confines of Barney Beck*

The broader track runs on across the moor, below one walled enclosure and above another, ignoring lesser branches before merging into a rough access road which runs to the farm buildings of Thirns just ahead. As it becomes surfaced to descend to Healaugh, instead take the left-hand access track climbing steeply to a cottage before continuing up to find level ground at a wall corner. Calver Hill forms a shapely crest above as the track runs across the moor with a wall for company. When the track finally turns in to a gate, a more inviting one continues on, soon rejoined by the wall to cross pleasantly along the moor edge, the heather now gone but the views remaining wide.

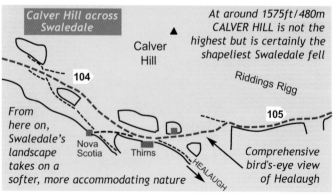

Calver Hill across Swaledale

Calver Hill ▲

At around 1575ft / 480m CALVER HILL is not the highest but is certainly the shapeliest Swaledale fell

Riddings Rigg

104

105

From here on, Swaledale's landscape takes on a softer, more accommodating nature

Nova Scotia

Thirns

HEALAUGH

Comprehensive bird's-eye view of Healaugh

94

Above the farm of Riddings the track drops gently down: as it becomes firmer and bends left, keep straight on the more inviting grassy path ahead to a prominent cairn just short of the next wall-corner. Just beyond is a recess and a gate where the hidden green way of Skelgate waits to deliver you into Reeth. Its enchanting start is soon overtaken by exuberant undergrowth, and as the walls are replaced by foliage the way becomes stonier underfoot. Just past a bend at a crossing farm track take a stile on the right, and slant left down through a gateway to a stile in the bottom corner behind the village school. Just below it a small gate puts you into a short snicket onto the valley road alongside the school. Go left on the footway down into the centre.

The green, Reeth

REETH is the capital of Swaledale within the National Park. It boasts an enviable position on the slopes of Calver Hill, well above the Swale and Arkle Beck. It is to the latter of these two watercourses it shows allegiance, with neighbouring Grinton claiming the Swale. Central is a large, sloping green, with the main buildings stood back on all sides. This old market town exudes a confident air, with hoary inns, shops, tearooms and Post office alongside the green: there is also a National Park Centre and craft centre. Reeth caters indiscriminately for dalesfolk and visitors alike: indelibly linked with the lead mining days, it was once much more populous. There is an absorbing folk museum, while annual agricultural shows and festivals add to its cultural attractions.

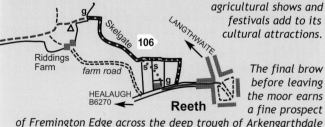

The final brow before leaving the moor earns a fine prospect of Fremington Edge across the deep trough of Arkengarthdale

10

REETH TO RICHMOND

DISTANCE 11 miles (17½km)   *ASCENT 900 feet/275m*

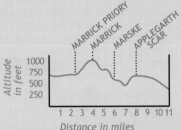

This easy section allows time to explore Richmond, though in truth one could devote a whole day to that. Within these few miles are an old priory, lovely villages, and a range of natural scenery from limestone scars and woodland to lush fields and leafy becks. The opening stage offers the only riverside section.

To lengthen the day consider going north from Reeth Bridge to Fremington Edge, and through Hurst and Washfold to the head of the Marske valley, then down this verdant vale to pick up the main route in Marske. A further departure would be a riverside path down from Applegarth to culminate on the opposite bank at

Richmond Bridge. A short variation early on is a nice path across the fields to Marrick Priory, above and parallel with the access road.

Ellers,
near Marrick

Leave by the main road at the bottom of the green, and shortly after crossing Reeth Bridge take a kissing-gate on the right. After passing a farm the enclosed path emerges into a field: it short-cuts Arkle Beck's confluence with the Swale by bearing across to a wall-corner, on to a kissing-gate and across to steps up onto Grinton Bridge. Grinton village is over it, but your route only crosses the road, where a path clings to the tree-lined river until emerging into the open. Here it is deflected by a wooded bank up onto the access road to Marrick Priory: turn right.

Today a tiny village, GRINTON was once the important centre for the dale. Its parish extended to the Westmorland border, and St Andrew's church, of Norman origin, is known as the 'Cathedral of the Dales'. Like Fremington a good Anglo-Saxon name, this is the only settlement of any size on the south side of the dale. At the centre of things is the busy Bridge Inn. Note also the mellow Blackburn Hall between church and river.

Reeth Bridge

Fremington

Arkle Beck

Reeth

Fremington Mill Farm
(former corn mill)

107

Grinton Br

On the moors above Grinton stands the castellated **Grinton +** Grinton Lodge, a shooting lodge turned youth hostel

MARRICK

former golf course

RICHMOND B6270

River Swale

108

The Swale at Grinton

The road runs unfailingly to Marrick Priory. After a cattle-grid by the buildings, take a gate on the left where a path rises to a bridle-gate into Steps Wood: a gem of a flagged path climbs through it. Leaving the wood a grass path remains with the right-hand wall as the going finally eases, and through a gate by a barn it continues as a grassy track to enter Marrick. Keep straight on past branches left and right, until the road swings left up to a T-junction with the 'main street'. Turn right past phone box and hall, and at the end, as the road swings left out of the village, take the 'no through road' right. Past the old school it loses its surface at a house behind: turn left up a grassy way behind it.

Ascend this short-lived way, becoming a path to a small gate at the top. Cross to a stile then up fieldsides with the village to the left. A couple of small enclosures are crossed, and finally away from the environs of Marrick's last house continuing along a fieldside. From a stile the thin path bears right through further stiles, over a brow then down to a gate onto a farm track with Nun Cote Nook to the left. Go right the few strides to the wall-corner, then drop to a gate by a barn. Continue down through a couple of wall-stiles to pass along the front of Ellers' garden wall.

Just behind turn down to a footbridge on Ellers Beck, then slant up through two fields onto Hollins Farm drive. Go briefly right then turn left up a short wallside track. Curve round to a gate/stile, then slant up to the wall opposite and over the brow to the far corner. From the stile advance a short way on the wallside to a gate in it, then cross a farm track and over the brow of the last field. Now angle left towards the wall to find a stile onto a road opposite a cottage. Turn right for a long descent to the bridge at the foot of Marske village.

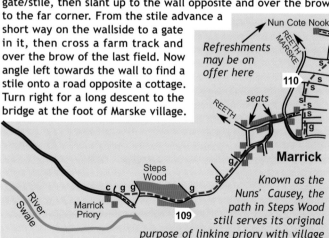

Nun Cote Nook

REETH MARSKE

Refreshments may be on offer here

110

REETH

seats

Marrick

Steps Wood

River Swale

Marrick Priory

109

Known as the Nuns' Causey, the path in Steps Wood still serves its original purpose of linking priory with village

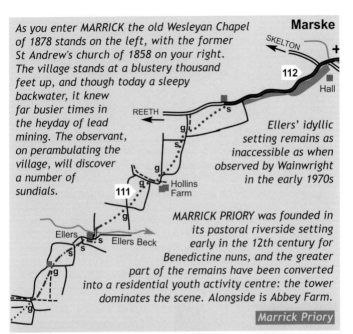

As you enter MARRICK the old Wesleyan Chapel of 1878 stands on the left, with the former St Andrew's church of 1858 on your right. The village stands at a blustery thousand feet up, and though today a sleepy backwater, it knew far busier times in the heyday of lead mining. The observant, on perambulating the village, will discover a number of sundials.

Marske

SKELTON

112

Hall

REETH

Ellers' idyllic setting remains as inaccessible as when observed by Wainwright in the early 1970s

Hollins Farm

111

Ellers   Ellers Beck

MARRICK PRIORY was founded in its pastoral riverside setting early in the 12th century for Benedictine nuns, and the greater part of the remains have been converted into a residential youth activity centre: the tower dominates the scene. Alongside is Abbey Farm.

Marrick Priory

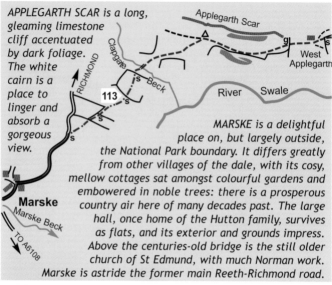

APPLEGARTH SCAR is a long, gleaming limestone cliff accentuated by dark foliage. The white cairn is a place to linger and absorb a gorgeous view.

MARSKE is a delightful place on, but largely outside, the National Park boundary. It differs greatly from other villages of the dale, with its cosy, mellow cottages sat amongst colourful gardens and embowered in noble trees: there is a prosperous country air here of many decades past. The large hall, once home of the Hutton family, survives as flats, and its exterior and grounds impress. Above the centuries-old bridge is the still older church of St Edmund, with much Norman work. Marske is astride the former main Reeth-Richmond road.

Cross Marske Bridge and rise past the church to a road junction, going right as far as the second bend in the road. Here a stile points the way through a string of hedges before the thin path drops down to a bridge over Clapgate Beck. A clear path slants up the opposite slope to a beckoning white-painted cairn alongside a farm road. Follow it right to West Applegarth and keep straight on to a wall-corner just beyond it. From a stile here a thin path crosses to another stile, from where a field is crossed to a stile to emerge on the drive to Low Applegarth.

High on the skyline above, WILLANCE'S LEAP is marked by no less than three monuments, and recalls an incident in 1606 when Robert Willance's horse careered over the cliff, killing itself in the process but leaving its rider with only a broken leg

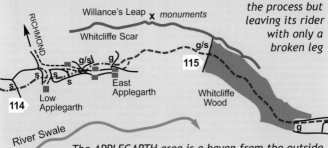

The APPLEGARTH area is a haven from the outside world. Its string of buildings occupy a green ledge beneath the scars and high above the Swale. The only road in is the narrow access road snaking down from the old Reeth-Richmond coach road. Here, between West and Low Applegarth, you vacate the Dales National Park. East Applegarth has a camping barn.

East Applegarth

Opposite: Marske church

Cross to a stile opposite and resume through one further stile and on near the front of High Applegarth to join the road serving East Applegarth. This is left within yards, however, as a gate/stile on the left point the way across a pasture above the farm. At a bridle-gate above it, a clearer path runs on to meet a cart track rising from the farm, and this runs a delightful course through rougher country to enter Whitcliffe Wood with its rich birdsong, ultimately re-emerging into scrub on the other side.

Richmond

The track runs on past High Leases, becoming surfaced for a long descent into Richmond. Above West Field you can opt for one of several stiles or gates to stroll along its top, returning to Westfields at the bottom corner to meet the road at the edge of town. Ideally, enter the Market Place by crossing the road to Cravengate, then along Finkle Street and Newbiggin.

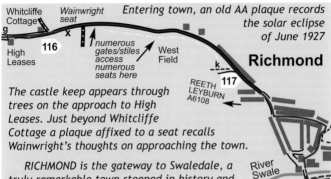

Entering town, an old AA plaque records the solar eclipse of June 1927

Whitcliffe Cottage
Wainwright seat
High Leases
116
numerous gates/stiles access
numerous seats here
West Field
Richmond

The castle keep appears through trees on the approach to High Leases. Just beyond Whitcliffe Cottage a plaque affixed to a seat recalls Wainwright's thoughts on approaching the town.

REETH
LEYBURN
A6108
117

River Swale

CATTERICK
CAMP A6136

RICHMOND is the gateway to Swaledale, a truly remarkable town steeped in history and dominated by its Norman castle high above the Swale. The well-preserved ruins are in the care of English Heritage: the enormous 12th century keep looks over the whole town including, almost at its feet, the Market Place. This equally enormous feature shares double bill with the castle, and has a multitude of uses. In the centre of its sloping cobbles is the Holy Trinity church with its 14th century tower: it uniquely incorporates a row of shops, and houses the Green Howards Museum. Lined by shops and pubs the Market Place is used as a bus station as well as for its original purpose on Saturdays: a market cross is still very much in evidence. Outside the square from which numerous wynds (narrow ways) radiate is St Mary's church, with 14th century tower and 16th century stalls. Also in the vicinity is Grey Friars Tower, across the road from the superbly restored and still functioning Georgian Theatre dating from 1788. The Culloden Tower stands nearer the river which flows between two graceful bridges. Richmond has an excellent information centre and even its own brewery, located with various other enterprises, including a cinema, in the splendidly restored railway station. The presence of the military around the town is due to the proximity of the massive Catterick Camp.

11

RICHMOND TO DANBY WISKE

DISTANCE 14³4 miles (23¹2km)   **ASCENT** 395 feet / 120m

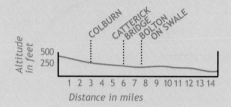

The near-marathon crossing of the Vale of Mowbray was originally the walk's longest stage, getting you from the Dales to the Moors in one fell swoop. Though certainly a worthy objective if you've a liking for elevated ground, a 23-mile day is beyond the pleasurable limits of most walkers, so here it is broken up into two albeit uneven sections. So though this stage is still a full day, you should hopefully be in reasonable shape if the previous day was only the suggested stroll from Reeth.

Features of interest largely come in the opening miles where the Swale itself provides early company. Beyond the Great North Road there are moments to break the monotony at Bolton on Swale, Bolton Beck and Kiplin Hall. The stage ends at Danby Wiske, the lowest point between the coasts but almost a Coast to Coast haven compared to Wainwright's 'slough of despond'.

Thanks to the opening up of rights of way that were once largely impassable, the once notorious amount of road walking has been considerably reduced - almost eradicated, in fact. Options to vary this stage are, unsurprisingly, very limited, save for a short refreshment detour to Scorton village, north of Bolton on Swale. One could get off to a flyer by eschewing the intricate early miles in favour of a route by way of Easby Abbey and Brompton on Swale: certainly Easby Abbey and its lovely environs deserve a visit.

From Castle Hill at the Market Place corner turn left off New Road to descend The Bar, under an arch and down Cornforth Hill to go left over Green (Richmond) Bridge. Turn downstream past sports fields into woodland, the main path soon rising into a field. Go left and locate a kissing-gate on the right, as a more obvious way runs on towards Mercury (Station) Bridge: your path rises between barns to a row of houses. At the main road go right, out of town. When it swings right after a private drive, a waterworks road doubles back left. At the works the path bears right outside its boundary and on into woodland above the river. Beyond a foot-bridge it climbs to leave the wood, and on to the rubble that was Hagg Farm. Go left on a stony track, fading at a gate where a thin trod rises across the field. Continue over the brow in the next field to a stile at the far corner, then bear left down a fieldside.

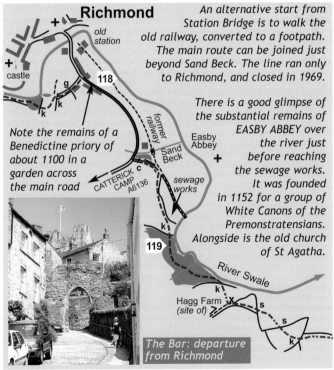

Richmond

old station

castle

118

g

k **k**

Note the remains of a Benedictine priory of about 1100 in a garden across the main road

former railway

CATTERICK CAMP A6136 **c**

Sand Beck

Easby Abbey

sewage works

119 **k**

An alternative start from Station Bridge is to walk the old railway, converted to a footpath. The main route can be joined just beyond Sand Beck. The line ran only to Richmond, and closed in 1969.

There is a good glimpse of the substantial remains of EASBY ABBEY over the river just before reaching the sewage works. It was founded in 1152 for a group of White Canons of the Premonstratensians. Alongside is the old church of St Agatha.

River Swale

k

Hagg Farm (site of) **X** **s**

s

k

The Bar: departure from Richmond

The Swale at St Giles

Down the field bear slightly right to a kissing-gate into the trees. A path accompanies Colburn Beck to emerge onto a drive, there turning right to enter sleepy Colburn. Cross the road bridge almost opposite and head along the street past the pub. At the end turn briefly right then left on a short access road by-passing the farm, and with the buildings to your left advance along a fieldside cart-track. At a second hedgerow take a branch left to approach a wooded bank above the river. Through a gate turn right to resume a fine stroll along a slender enclosure, through a bridle-gate at the end then veer gradually right to by-pass St Giles Farm and emerge onto its drive.

ST GILES HOSPITAL was one of a number run under monastic orders, and dates from the late 12th century. Excavations in 1990 revealed skeletons galore - removed to York for further research before river erosion washed it away! By the riverbank are the scant remains of the chapel, while on the banktop are numerous grassy earthworks of ancillary buildings. The site was abandoned over 500 years ago, though was later occupied by a farm, forerunner of the present one up above.

River Swale

Colburn Beck

121

x site of hospital

s

St Giles Farm

Hall

g

120 k

Colburn

TO A6136

Acquaintance with COLBURN is limited to the old village, to which a larger, modern appendage has been added nearer Catterick Camp. Village pub is the Hildyard Arms, while the hall is a fine old manor house. On leaving note the unusual architectural merit of the range of old farm outbuildings alongside.

106

Catterick Bridge

Almost at once go left through a small gate above a wooded bank, and from one at the end head along a gentle bank top, largely a super green way to Thornbrough. Keeping left of the buildings, drop left to discover the pulsating A1 just below! Pass under this and an old rail bridge to rise slightly right to a stile onto the old A1 opposite the racecourse at Catterick Bridge. Cross with care to the hotel and then left over the bridge. From a stile on the right a path heads downstream, never far from the Swale's bank, and passing a crumbling wall thought to be of Roman origin. Beyond a scrubby area the bank opens out.

At CATTERICK BRIDGE the Romans had a military settlement Cataractonium astride their road of Dere Street. This important river crossing was also recognised in coaching days, the house by the bridge once being a smithy. Alongside are refreshments at the Bridge Hotel.

Brompton on Swale B6271

A6136

pond in old gravel pit

123

River Swale

old railway bridge

A1

s s s

Catterick Bridge

122

g

The skeleton rail bridge over the Swale carried a military line to Catterick Camp

g

Thornbrough Farm camping

CATTERICK CAMP A6136

CATTERICK A6136

race course

The A1 by-passed Catterick in 1959

Catterick is just one of a string of famous racecourses in Yorkshire's 'low' country

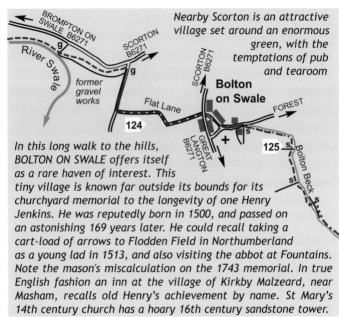

Nearby Scorton is an attractive village set around an enormous green, with the temptations of pub and tearoom

In this long walk to the hills, BOLTON ON SWALE offers itself as a rare haven of interest. This tiny village is known far outside its bounds for its churchyard memorial to the longevity of one Henry Jenkins. He was reputedly born in 1500, and passed on an astonishing 169 years later. He could recall taking a cart-load of arrows to Flodden Field in Northumberland as a young lad in 1513, and also visiting the abbot at Fountains. Note the mason's miscalculation on the 1743 memorial. In true English fashion an inn at the village of Kirkby Malzeard, near Masham, recalls old Henry's achievement by name. St Mary's 14th century church has a hoary 16th century sandstone tower.

Remain on the pleasant riverbank to the end, where a bridle-gate sends a path through a scrubby area that not long ago was a gravel works. It deposits you at the end onto a side road: turn right, and at the first chance go left on a rough lane to emerge onto the B6271 at Bolton on Swale. Cross straight over and head for the church, passing the preserved village pump en route.

At the church go briefly left on the road, an early stile on the right pointing you to Bolton Beck. Accompany this charming stream through the fields, crossing it at an old stone bridge. Resume upstream across a farm drive and along to a stile onto a road. Go briefly left, rising to Ellerton Hill. Turn right on the drive past houses old and new, and through a gate/stile a hedgeside path runs to a stile then a bridle-gate back onto the B6271. Turn left on the verge, passing Kiplin Hall and a branch left. A little further the road swings sharp right: here take a gate on the left and escape along a pleasant drive to isolated Ladybank House.

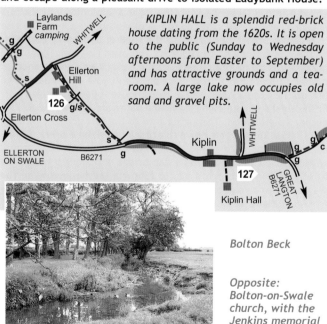

KIPLIN HALL is a splendid red-brick house dating from the 1620s. It is open to the public (Sunday to Wednesday afternoons from Easter to September) and has attractive grounds and a tea-room. A large lake now occupies old sand and gravel pits.

Bolton Beck

Opposite:
Bolton-on-Swale
church, with the
Jenkins memorial

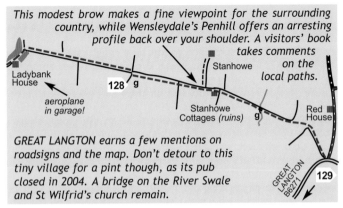

This modest brow makes a fine viewpoint for the surrounding country, while Wensleydale's Penhill offers an arresting profile back over your shoulder. A visitors' book takes comments on the local paths.

Ladybank House

aeroplane in garage!

128 g

Stanhowe

Stanhowe Cottages (ruins)

9

Red House

GREAT LANGTON earns a few mentions on roadsigns and the map. Don't detour to this tiny village for a pint though, as its pub closed in 2004. A bridge on the River Swale and St Wilfrid's church remain.

GREAT LANGTON B6271

129

Keep on past the house and a path runs through greenery to emerge into a large field. To the right a splendid path starts a bee-line, at the end crossing to the other side of a hedge to rise to a gentle brow, then down to the shell of Stanhowe Cottages. At the end a stone bridge conveys you over The Stell. When the hedge turns off up the other side, the path bears right to another corner to lead out onto a junction. Don't join the road but go left on the access road, and at Moor House follow its drive right. From a gate on the right leave the farmyard and advance to a corner stile beyond. Through a gate to the left go right through a stile then slightly left down to a plank bridge on a drain. A field centre path heads away to another stile and on through a very wide field. At the end cross a slab bridge and along a hedgeside briefly, passing through a gap to follow a tall hedgerow all the way down to a road opposite Brock Holme Farm.

Turn right a short way then left on the drive to High Brockholme. When it swings right to the farm take a bridle-gate in front, and on to another in a kink just ahead. Through this follow a long hedgerow descending very gently to the bottom of the field, passing through a gate/stile and going briefly left to the corner. Don't pass through but turn right up the hedgeside, and along to a gate/stile into an enclosed green way, a delight-ful stroll of prolonged greenery before emerging at the far end with Danby Wiske part of a sweeping view just ahead. Follow the fieldside left to join a cart track curving round to emerge onto a road. Go left into the village.

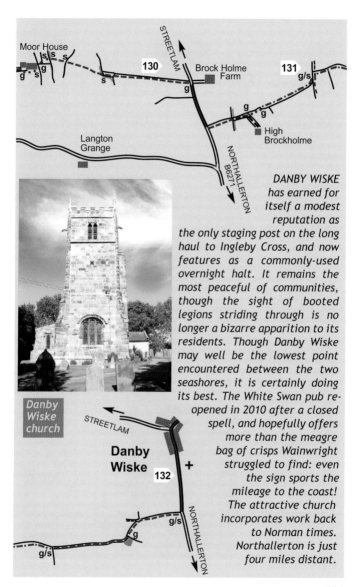

Moor House

STREETLAM

130

Brock Holme Farm

131

Langton Grange

High Brockholme

NORTHALLERTON B6271

Danby Wiske church

DANBY WISKE has earned for itself a modest reputation as the only staging post on the long haul to Ingleby Cross, and now features as a commonly-used overnight halt. It remains the most peaceful of communities, though the sight of booted legions striding through is no longer a bizarre apparition to its residents. Though Danby Wiske may well be the lowest point encountered between the two seashores, it is certainly doing its best. The White Swan pub re-opened in 2010 after a closed spell, and hopefully offers more than the meagre bag of crisps Wainwright struggled to find: even the sign sports the mileage to the coast! The attractive church incorporates work back to Norman times. Northallerton is just four miles distant.

STREETLAM

Danby Wiske

132

NORTHALLERTON

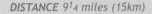

12

DANBY WISKE TO INGLEBY CROSS

DISTANCE 9¼ miles (15km)   **ASCENT** 265 feet/80m

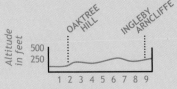

The easiest section on offer concludes the crossing of the Vale of Mowbray, leaving behind the lowest point between the coasts for the fringe of the North York Moors - the start of the last, exhilarating lap. The walking is unspectacular but largely off-road and generally very pleasant as you traverse quiet farmland in readiness for the Moors.

There are no outstanding options to vary the route, though it would be possible to curve north via the villages of Deighton, Welbury, West and East Rounton; or possibly south via Brompton and East Harlsey: this might be useful if you've overnighted in Northallerton. If bound for Osmotherley, you could shorten things by leaving Long Lane in favour of a route by Low Moor and Harlsey Castle. A rewarding visit to Mount Grace Priory and its lovely environs might also then be incorporated.

Mount Grace Priory

Leave Danby by keeping straight on the road past the pub, bridging the snaking River Wiske and, a little beyond, the East Coast railway line. Leave the road at a gate on the left opposite a drive to Lazenby Hall Farm. Passing through a thicket, a path slants right across the field to the far corner: continue away along the hedgeside, through an intervening stile.

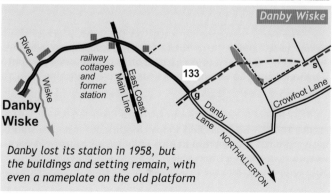

Danby lost its station in 1958, but the buildings and setting remain, with even a nameplate on the old platform

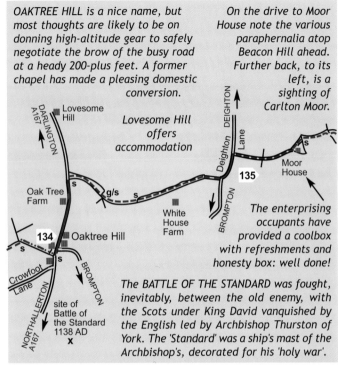

OAKTREE HILL is a nice name, but most thoughts are likely to be on donning high-altitude gear to safely negotiate the brow of the busy road at a heady 200-plus feet. A former chapel has made a pleasing domestic conversion.

On the drive to Moor House note the various paraphernalia atop Beacon Hill ahead. Further back, to its left, is a sighting of Carlton Moor.

Lovesome Hill offers accommodation

The enterprising occupants have provided a coolbox with refreshments and honesty box: well done!

The BATTLE OF THE STANDARD was fought, inevitably, between the old enemy, with the Scots under King David vanquished by the English led by Archbishop Thurston of York. The 'Standard' was a ship's mast of the Archbishop's, decorated for his 'holy war'.

After a second stile go right with a hedge to join the A167 alongside Oak Tree Garage. Cross and go left on the verge past Oak Tree Farm to escape by a stile on the right. A grassy track heads away, and a little further a continuing path becomes enclosed by greenery to run a delightful course emerging onto Deighton Lane. Go left only as far as a drive branching right to Moor House. Pass left of all the buildings to a corner stile, and away along a fieldside. Through a hedge-gap bear right with another hedge to bridge a drain at a gate. Bear left across a field centre to a corner stile and simple footbridge, then rise gently away towards the hotch-potch of buildings of Northfield Farm. Keep left of them all to a stile, then straight ahead to the next stile to join the farm road. Go left past Northfield House and out along the access road onto another road.

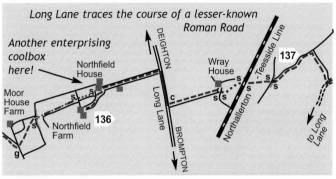

Long Lane traces the course of a lesser-known Roman Road

Another enterprising coolbox here!

Northfield House

Moor House Farm

Northfield Farm

136

DEIGHTON

Long Lane

BROMPTON

Wray House

Teesside Line

137

Northallerton

to Long Lane

Deep in the Vale of Mowbray

Turn briefly right then go left along the drive to Wray House. Again neatly avoiding a farmyard, go right down a short way into a field with a railway ahead. Bear well to the left to cross with care, then head straight down the field to a footbridge and then a plank in a field corner. Its boundary is now followed left around two sides to join the surfaced Low Moor Lane: go left.

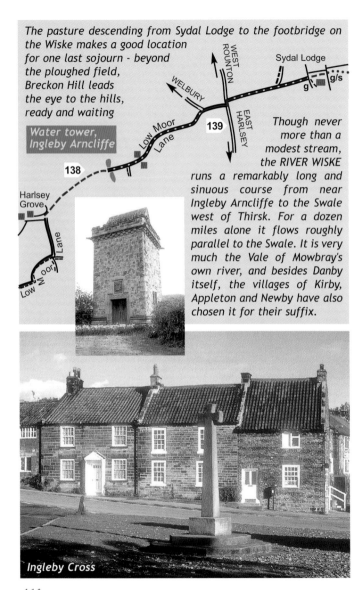

The pasture descending from Sydal Lodge to the footbridge on the Wiske makes a good location for one last sojourn - beyond the ploughed field, Breckon Hill leads the eye to the hills, ready and waiting

WEST ROUNTON

Sydal Lodge

WELBURY

EAST HARLSEY

Low Moor Lane

139

Water tower, Ingleby Arncliffe

138

Harlsey Grove

Low Moor Lane

Though never more than a modest stream, the RIVER WISKE runs a remarkably long and sinuous course from near Ingleby Arncliffe to the Swale west of Thirsk. For a dozen miles alone it flows roughly parallel to the Swale. It is very much the Vale of Mowbray's own river, and besides Danby itself, the villages of Kirby, Appleton and Newby have also chosen it for their suffix.

Ingleby Cross

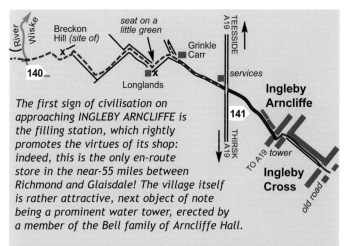

The first sign of civilisation on approaching INGLEBY ARNCLIFFE is the filling station, which rightly promotes the virtues of its shop: indeed, this is the only en-route store in the near-55 miles between Richmond and Glaisdale! The village itself is rather attractive, next object of note being a prominent water tower, erected by a member of the Bell family of Arncliffe Hall.

Long since gratefully by-passed, INGLEBY CROSS is the 'business' partner, now minus its tiny store. Its 'cross' (war memorial), its Blue Bell Inn, its village hall and its cottages all enjoy a peace disturbed only by the occasional Northallerton-Stokesley bus and the exhausted walkers abandoned on its welcoming green.

Low Moor Lane runs on to approach the farmstead of Harlsey Grove, and when it turns in to it, bear right on the rougher continuation. A long trek along Low Moor Lane leads out to a surfaced road. Go right to a junction then left, only to turn right almost at once along the drive to Sydal Lodge. Go straight ahead at the house and on towards farm buildings, but then keep straight on again to a gate. The path heads away with the ruin of Breckon Hill a sure guide straight ahead, and the Cleveland Hills now almost touchable behind.

The path descends to a footbridge (the lazy Wiske again) and then climbs to Breckon Hill, passing right of the crumbling remains to follow the drive out. The buzz of traffic on the A19 is heard as the drive zigzags past two farms to emerge onto the highway alongside a filling station and cafe. A dual carriageway is of benefit (as you need only look one way at once) on this final hairy crossing to a contrastingly narrow lane running into Ingleby Arncliffe. At the staggered junction keep on to descend Cross Lane into adjoining Ingleby Cross.

13

INGLEBY CROSS TO CLAY BANK TOP

DISTANCE 12 miles (19km)   *ASCENT 2700 feet/825m*

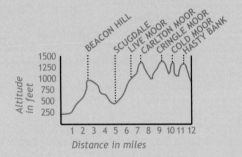

Growing ever nearer over the last miles, the Cleveland Hills are now underfoot, and this is truly a day to savour, incorporating the most famous dozen miles on the North York Moors. Throughout the crossing of the escarpment are superb views not only out to the Cleveland Plain and into the heart of the moors, but also of the day's hills' ever-changing aspects. Though the miles are few and the route clear, this is quite a roller-coaster. Rather than trying to press on beyond Clay Bank Top, it is firmly recommended to take your time, perhaps include a visit to the majestic Mount Grace Priory, and finish with a downhill stroll (or lift) into Great Broughton. With luck your host will deposit you back on Clay Bank Top after breakfast.

A lower level alternative exists by using lanes and field-paths north of the great escarpment, by way of Swainby, Faceby and Carlton. The route could be picked up on Carlton Bank to follow the jet miners' track (see map). If passing over Clay Bank Top is not important, then a further option cuts through Scugdale and over the top to Chop Gate, there taking a track onto Urra Moor to pick up the route on Round Hill.

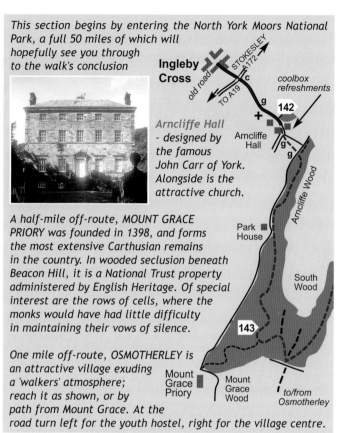

This section begins by entering the North York Moors National Park, a full 50 miles of which will hopefully see you through to the walk's conclusion

Ingleby Cross

STOKESLEY
A172
old road
TO A19
c

coolbox refreshments

g
142

Arncliffe Hall - designed by the famous John Carr of York. Alongside is the attractive church.

Arncliffe Hall

g
g

Arncliffe Wood

A half-mile off-route, MOUNT GRACE PRIORY was founded in 1398, and forms the most extensive Carthusian remains in the country. In wooded seclusion beneath Beacon Hill, it is a National Trust property administered by English Heritage. Of special interest are the rows of cells, where the monks would have had little difficulty in maintaining their vows of silence.

Park House

South Wood

143

One mile off-route, OSMOTHERLEY is an attractive village exuding a 'walkers' atmosphere; reach it as shown, or by path from Mount Grace. At the road turn left for the youth hostel, right for the village centre.

Mount Grace Priory

Mount Grace Wood

to/from Osmotherley

From the green head past the Blue Bell out onto the A172. Cross over and along the leafy lane past Arncliffe church and Hall, then up the hill take a gate on the left to follow a track up into Arncliffe Wood. Turn right along the forest road, passing above Park House and soon climbing deeper into the woods. The way remains clear, swinging up to a T-junction and there rising right to the wood edge. The gate in front signals your merging with the Cleveland Way coming out from Osmotherley, but without leaving the wood turn sharply up to the left on a clear, much nicer path rising above a forest road through South Wood.

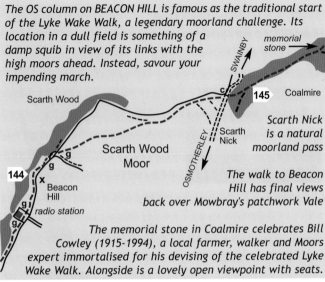

The OS column on BEACON HILL is famous as the traditional start of the Lyke Wake Walk, a legendary moorland challenge. Its location in a dull field is something of a damp squib in view of its links with the high moors ahead. Instead, savour your impending march.

memorial stone

Coalmire

Scarth Wood

Scarth Wood Moor

Scarth Nick

Scarth Nick is a natural moorland pass

The walk to Beacon Hill has final views back over Mowbray's patchwork Vale

Beacon Hill

radio station

The memorial stone in Coalmire celebrates Bill Cowley (1915-1994), a local farmer, walker and Moors expert immortalised for his devising of the celebrated Lyke Wake Walk. Alongside is a lovely open viewpoint with seats.

At the top of the wood the path runs along a wallside, past an incongruous BT microwave radio station and an easily-missed Ordnance Survey column atop Beacon Hill. A little beyond, the way emerges onto a corner of Scarth Wood Moor, a glorious moment. In the distance is the famous conical peak of Roseberry Topping, but nearer to hand is a striking array of moors that form the greater part of the day - an exciting prospect indeed.

The main path crosses the moor diagonally to descend by a wall onto the road through Scarth Nick, and across the cattle-grid take a path into the plantation. This quickly joins a forest road through Coalmire, which is left at a memorial stone on a footpath dropping steeply left. At a staggered crossroads go left a couple of steps and then sharply right, a clear path running along the foot of Clain Wood. In lovely surroundings a kissing-gate on the left signals time to leave by descending a field into trees, and a rough track fords a small stream (footbridge too). On the other side a narrow road fords Scugdale Beck (footbridge again) and leads up to the left past a farm to a junction at Huthwaite Green. Cross straight over and up an enclosed path ahead, swinging left along the base of a plantation.

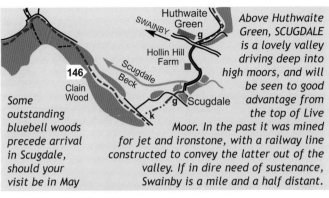

Above Huthwaite Green, SCUGDALE is a lovely valley driving deep into high moors, and will be seen to good advantage from the top of Live Moor. In the past it was mined for jet and ironstone, with a railway line constructed to convey the latter out of the valley. If in dire need of sustenance, Swainby is a mile and a half distant.

Some outstanding bluebell woods precede arrival in Scugdale, should your visit be in May

Springtime in Scugdale

Further along, a bridle-gate admits to a steep climb through the trees. The open moor is quickly gained, and a pleasant climb eases out over the brow of Live Moor. The path runs past its sprawling summit cairn and up onto waiting Carlton Moor: the final section is sandwiched between the escarpment to the left and a glider runway to the right. The summit is marked by an Ordnance Survey column and a tall boundary stone, a good place to halt. On a clear day you might have a view of the sea, north-wards beyond the industry of Teesside!

On the steep descent the path has been re-routed away from precipitous drops into alum quarries that scar the northern face of the hill. The gliding club access road is crossed to meet the Carlton-Chop Gate road on Carlton Bank (cafe just to right). Across, a path runs between clumps of trees: on opening out take the right fork for a short pull towards the waiting Cringle End.

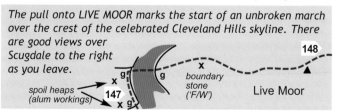

The pull onto LIVE MOOR marks the start of an unbroken march over the crest of the celebrated Cleveland Hills skyline. There are good views over Scugdale to the right as you leave.

148

x

spoil heaps (alum workings)

147

boundary stone ('F/W')

Live Moor

Boundary stone on Live Moor

Opposite: Cringle Moor from Carlton Moor

On CARLTON BANK a minor road cuts through the hills: a welcome feature is a cafe concealed in the hillside. On the roadside above, four large stones mark a prehistoric burial mound.

From Live Moor to CARLTON MOOR the track is visible all the way ahead, the steep western flank contrasting with the heather carpet of the moortop. In the fashion of its ensuing colleagues, Carlton Moor rises gently from the south to an abrupt terminus overlooking the Cleveland Plain. Select a heathery couch, and with the aid of a map try to identify the villages outspread. The nearest, fittingly, is Carlton.

CARLTON

Carlton Bank

cafe

150

CHOP GATE

OS column

△ Carlton Moor

149

glider runway

■ Gliding Club

Faceby Bank

Gold Hill

Holey Moor

x *fading white painted boundary stone ('A/F')*

The jet and alum workings that litter these escarpments are at their most evident in the alum ravaged cliffs on Carlton Bank

Carlton Moor GLIDING CLUB is an astonishing sight to first-time visitors on the top of the iconic Cleveland Hills. Though long-established it ceased activities in 2008, and it is to be hoped its bulldozed runway and ramshackle hangar will be duly removed.

Cringle Moor

Above: Carlton Moor from Cringle End

Left: Cold Moor from Cringle

Below (both): On Cringle End

Arrival on CRINGLE END is a champagne moment: aside from the ever-present views over the Cleveland Plain to the peak of Roseberry Topping, the highlight is the sudden appearance of Cringle's northern slopes plunging dramatically to the lower contours, with both Cold Moor and Hasty Bank making their appearances in some style. The furniture of view indicator, seat and boundary stone confirms this as a compulsory halt, one of those indefinable 'good places to be'. The view indicator is a memorial to a much respected local rambler and writer.

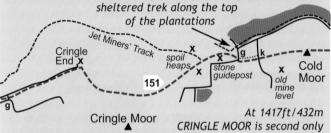

The lower-level track can be picked up in this gap for a more sheltered trek along the top of the plantations

Jet Miners' Track

Cringle End

spoil heaps

stone guidepost

151

old mine level

Cold Moor

Cringle Moor ▲

At 1417ft/432m CRINGLE MOOR is second only to Urra Moor's Round Hill in the hierarchy of the Moors, yet its summit is the only one along this escarpment that is omitted, being set well back amidst heather

COLD MOOR points a slender finger south to Bilsdale, and from its tiny cairn at 1319ft/402m an inviting path sets off through the heather. Along with ironstone and alum, these hills were also plundered for jet (of 'jet black' fame), a once-popular ornamental stone. Evidence of the mines is most apparent when looking back to Cringle from Cold Moor.

Guidepost under Cringle Moor

Cringle End is gained at a boundary stone, view indicator and seat. The path rises a little further, dramatically along the escarpment just below Cringle Moor's summit. A steep descent follows down to the depression in front of Cold Moor, where an old wall is followed up then crossed for the short climb to its cairn.

The Wainstones

The approach
from Garfit Gap

At The
Wainstones

Looking back to
appropriately
named Cold Moor

CLAY BANK TOP is a major breach in the moorland dome, its crest at some 870ft/265m exploited by the only notable north-south road to cross the western half of these uplands. To the south Bilsdale and Ryedale lead ultimately to the market town of Helmsley, but most folk settle for a walk or lift northwards to Great Broughton.

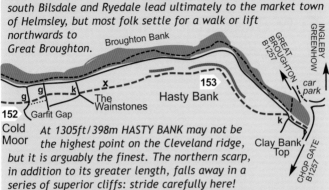

Cold Moor

At 1305ft/398m HASTY BANK may not be the highest point on the Cleveland ridge, but it is arguably the finest. The northern scarp, in addition to its greater length, falls away in a series of superior cliffs: stride carefully here!

THE WAINSTONES are Hasty Bank's pride and joy, a tumble of crags and boulders certain to rejuvenate even the most ancient among us, and of sufficient substance to regularly attract rock climbers. They form an enduring Cleveland Hills landmark.

Urra Moor across Clay Bank Top from Hasty Bank

The descent from Cold Moor to Garfit Gap is equally rapid, spurred on by the prospect of the Wainstones on Hasty Bank, the final summit before Clay Bank Top. A short pull is followed by an easy clamber up between the pinnacles, and then a lengthy crossing of Hasty Bank's broad top. When its steep northern scarp subsides, the inevitable steep descent runs down to the top of the plantations that cloak the northern slopes, and a wall-side path drops the final steps onto the road summit.

14

CLAY BANK TOP TO ROSEDALE HEAD

DISTANCE 10½ miles (17km)   *ASCENT 965 feet/295m*

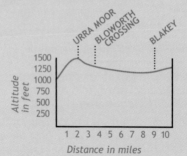

Considering that almost all of this stage is spent above the 1250ft contour, the walking is supremely effortless. Only the first half-mile pull onto Urra Moor offers any resistance, after which broad strides, broad tracks and even broader sweeps of moorland are the order of the day. Beyond the summit of the moors on Round Hill, the Rosedale ironstone railway trackbed is picked up at Bloworth Crossing, and winds a well-engineered course around the head of Farndale before throwing you off at Blakey. Here the Lion Inn awaits your thirst, and with its only neighbour for miles just across the road, makes Blakey a memorable spot to pass a night. For neatness the section continues a little further to the heart of the moors at Rosedale Head. The road through Blakey and Rosedale Head is a popular north-south moorland crossing, giving opportunity to find a lift either north to Castleton or south to Hutton-le-Hole for accommodation.

Though many will forge on from Rosedale Head down the easy miles into Glaisdale, those ending their day at Blakey could opt to vary it by devising more circuitous routes delving either north into Westerdale, the very head of Eskdale, or more invitingly south into Farndale.

Leave the road summit opposite where you arrived, and a wide path rises, fairly steeply in the earlier stages, onto the heather of Urra Moor. After a mile and a half lined by cairns and boundary stones the Ordnance Survey column on Round Hill is reached, just off to the left from the Hand Stone.

On Urra Moor:
The Hand Stone,
The Face Stone

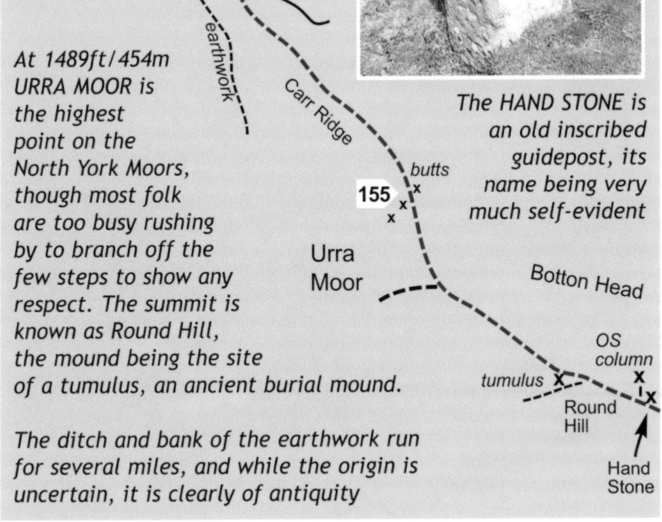

At 1489ft / 454m URRA MOOR is the highest point on the North York Moors, though most folk are too busy rushing by to branch off the few steps to show any respect. The summit is known as Round Hill, the mound being the site of a tumulus, an ancient burial mound.

The ditch and bank of the earthwork run for several miles, and while the origin is uncertain, it is clearly of antiquity

The HAND STONE is an old inscribed guidepost, its name being very much self-evident

Clay Bank Top

earthwork

Carr Ridge

butts

Urra Moor

Botton Head

tumulus

OS column

Round Hill

Hand Stone

From Bloworth Crossing to beneath the Lion Inn on Blakey Ridge, you follow the trackbed of the ROSEDALE IRONSTONE RAILWAY. It was built in 1861 to convey ironstone from Rosedale, in the heart of the moors, out over the watershed and down to the furnaces of Teesside. This remarkable feat of engineering saw trains cross the moors at some 1300ft/396m. The line closed in 1929, and today it is difficult to visualise either the trains or the thousands labouring hard in now tranquil Rosedale.

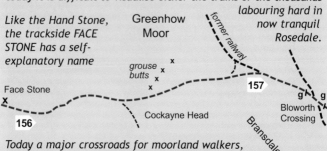

Like the Hand Stone, the trackside FACE STONE has a self-explanatory name

Greenhow Moor

former railway

grouse butts

Face Stone

157

Bloworth Crossing

156

Cockayne Head

Bransdale

Today a major crossroads for moorland walkers, BLOWORTH CROSSING was a true crossing in railway days. The Rudland Rigg road that crosses here was also of great significance in times past, an important highway over the moors evidenced by centuries-old inscribed stones along its route.

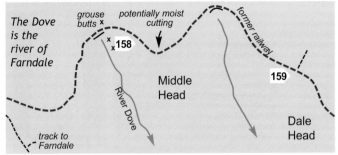

The Dove is the river of Farndale

grouse butts x

x x158

potentially moist cutting

former railway

River Dove

Middle Head

159

Dale Head

track to Farndale

Beyond Round Hill the track makes a dignified descent to merge with the trackbed of the old Rosedale Ironstone Railway, whose course will be discerned well before it is joined. Turn right along it, and only a little further you reach Bloworth Crossing, a major moorland crossroads. Here take your leave of the Cleveland Way, which turns sharply to follow the old road north, while you now take advantage of the trackbed for no less than five miles further, contouring around the head of Farndale and its many infant streams.

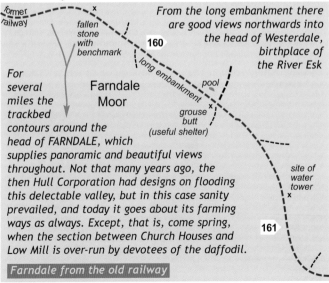

former railway

fallen stone with benchmark

160

long embankment

From the long embankment there are good views northwards into the head of Westerdale, birthplace of the River Esk

pool

grouse butt (useful shelter)

For several miles the trackbed contours around the head of FARNDALE, which supplies panoramic and beautiful views throughout. Not that many years ago, the then Hull Corporation had designs on flooding this delectable valley, but in this case sanity prevailed, and today it goes about its farming ways as always. Except, that is, come spring, when the section between Church Houses and Low Mill is over-run by devotees of the daffodil.

site of water tower x

161

Farndale Moor

Farndale from the old railway

131

Inscribed stones,
Rosedale Head

At a final cutting the Lion Inn at Blakey appears inspiringly on the skyline, and the head of one last side-valley is rounded before a path strikes off left to climb through heather up to a wallside and the standing stone on Blakey Howe, immediately above the pub. Beyond the moor road is the head of Rosedale, and while the rail track heads that way, it does so without you. Few will resist a break at the Lion, first opportunity for en-route alcoholic refreshment since Ingleby Cross. On emerging blinking into the daylight, turn north on the capacious verge for a mile as far as a large, ungainly stone on the left known as Margery Bradley. A path now strikes off right through heather, cutting the corner of the road junction at Rosedale Head to meet the Rosedale Abbey road at the prominent guide of White Cross.

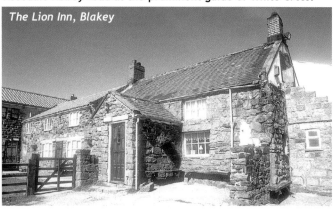

The Lion Inn, Blakey

The LION INN dates back over 400 years, and once frequented by ironstone and coal miners, today it is a prominent and hugely popular landmark waylaying walkers and tourists. The highway it serves carries a surprising volume of traffic for a humble moorland road: the answer lies in it being a rare link between villages in the north and south of the Park, with neither severe gradients nor bends. South of the Lion is Blakey Junction, where the former railway divided for either Rosedale West Mines, or to encircle Rosedale Head for several miles more to Rosedale East Mines.

ROSEDALE HEAD was - and still is - an important meeting place of moorland roads and tracks. Iconic Ralph Cross was adopted as the National Park's symbol, but has been subject to toppling by vandals. It's not all glory!

At just under 1312ft/400m the Lion's lofty and windswept altitude coincides with that of Bloworth Crossing

The burial mound on Blakey Howe was later used for cockfighting - the pit is still evident

WESTERDALE

CASTLETON

also known as Fat Betty

White Cross

Ralph Cross x

x Old Ralph

Rosedale Head

old coal pits

164

boundary stones inscribed Westerdale & Spaunton

Margery Bradley

x inscribed stone

River Seven

boundary stone

163

former railway

guidestone ('Rosedale Rode North')

Blakey Howe

High Blakey Moor

162

former railway

Blakey Gill

Lion Inn camping

Blakey

HUTTON-LE-HOLE

The Lion Inn makes its welcome skyline appearance

15

Rosedale Head to Grosmont

DISTANCE 12½ miles (20km)   **ASCENT** 315 feet/96m

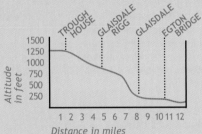

With its high-altitude start the walking on this section is again effortless, with further broad strides, broad tracks and even broader sweeps of moorland! Beyond the heart of the moors at Rosedale Head, with its crosses and various stones, the way encircles the magnificent head of Great Fryup Dale, a tributary of the Esk to which the long declining miles of Glaisdale Rigg will ultimately lead. Once in Eskdale a delightful amble incorporates an old paved trod through delectable woodland, a second lovely village and a conclusion along an old toll road.

Any number of more circuitous alternatives can be devised by breaking off earlier from Danby High Moor for Eskdale, either into Danby Dale or Great Fryup Dale and thence via Lealholm.

White Cross (Fat Betty),
Rosedale Head

Though the shooters' cabin of TROUGH HOUSE is likely to be locked, it does offer a welcome seat to appraise impending Great Fryup

The continuation of Danby High Moor is DANBY RIGG, which slims substantially on its descent to Eskdale, and bears the remains of hundreds of burial cairns dating back to Bronze Age times

Danby High Moor

DANBY

old pits

Trough House **166**

g

Danby Head

From DANBY HIGH MOOR there **165** are views west beyond the head of Eskdale to Roseberry Topping. While crossing these broadest of acres, it won't be difficult to appreciate why late summer is the finest time to be here.

All of this terrain is the centre of a great moorland dome, in general being little more than 100ft/30m below the moors' highest point

ROSEDALE ABBEY

Trough House

The route turns right for ten minutes until a thin but clear path branches left, short-cutting a road junction to emerge on the narrow Little Fryup Dale road. This is accompanied left over a gentle brow with Eskdale outspread far ahead, and as Trough House appears, a broad track soon branches off for it. Remain on this past the stone hut towards the head of Great Fryup Dale.

Beyond the hut you encounter the headwaters of Great Fryup Beck, the way 'narrowing' into a broad path that encircles the head of Great Fryup Dale in style. This is a splendid section, with many miles of heather surrounds enhanced by the addition of bilberry and some bracken, while the colourful and rough-fashioned dalehead drops steeply away to the left. Continuing on, the broad path eventually filters onto a moorland road. Turn left for a mile as far as a broad track branching straight ahead as the road swings left to a white Ordnance Survey column. This is the old road along Glaisdale Rigg, and is followed unerringly all the way down towards its village, a super promenade.

Great Fryup Dale from Great Fryup Head

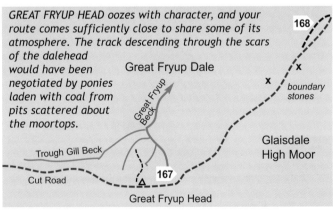

GREAT FRYUP HEAD oozes with character, and your route comes sufficiently close to share some of its atmosphere. The track descending through the scars of the dalehead would have been negotiated by ponies laden with coal from pits scattered about the moortops.

168

Great Fryup Dale

x   x

boundary stones

Great Fryup Beck

Glaisdale High Moor

Trough Gill Beck

Cut Road

167

Great Fryup Head

GLAISDALE RIGG is only one of a string of moorland ridges lining the south side of Eskdale, but it is by far the finest for walkers by virtue of the old road running throughout its length

A bounty of inscribed guidestones testifies to the historical significance of the Rigg road

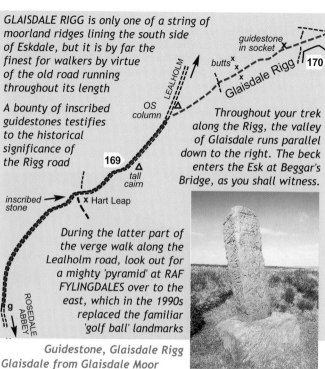

guidestone in socket X

butts X
X
X

Glaisdale Rigg

170

LEALHOLM

OS column

△

169
△
tall cairn

inscribed stone →
X Hart Leap

Throughout your trek along the Rigg, the valley of Glaisdale runs parallel down to the right. The beck enters the Esk at Beggar's Bridge, as you shall witness.

During the latter part of the verge walk along the Lealholm road, look out for a mighty 'pyramid' at RAF FYLINGDALES over to the east, which in the 1990s replaced the familiar 'golf ball' landmarks

g
ROSEDALE ABBEY

Guidestone, Glaisdale Rigg
Glaisdale from Glaisdale Moor

Heather moor gives way to grass moor as height is lost, with the broad Eskdale scene increasing in clarity. Eventually the old road meets a surfaced lanehead to drop onto a green at the head of Glaisdale. Several permutations of route lead from here to the railway station at the village foot, and these may depend upon whether you're seeking lodgings. All steps first turn right, the finest route turning left down a side road by the phone box, at the end of the terrace containing the shop. Winding down to the river (with first glimpses of the River Esk) it runs a delightful valley floor course to emerge on the main road opposite the pub. Turn left to the station at Beggar's Bridge.

Guidestone, Glaisdale Rigg

River Esk, Glaisdale

seat
X
g

Glaisdale
Low Moor

171

This prominent embankment belongs to a long-departed tramway to an ironstone mine

X
X
X   boundary
    stones

X standing stone

Glaisdale Rigg

Opposite: Beggar's Bridge, Glaisdale

GLAISDALE is a scattered village comprising of three distinct corners spreading from the environs of Beggar's Bridge up to the very edge of breezy Glaisdale Rigg. At the foot of its substantial side valley, it boasts both fragrant woods and rolling moors on its doorstep, and typifies the lovely Esk Valley in its commendable attempts to deter the motor car from making logical progress: truly the railway is a necessity here.

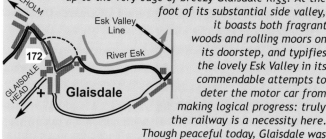

Though peaceful today, Glaisdale was caught up in the 19th century iron ore 'boom' - when mining was in full swing one of its hostelries underwent a name change to the 'Three Blast Furnaces', which were operating nearby. Until quite recently the village still boasted three pubs, but the Mitre Tavern and the Anglers Rest have left just the Arncliffe Arms to slake thirsts - note that this is found at the bottom (eastern) end. An equally invaluable Post office/store also survives.

*The Horseshoe,
Egton Bridge*

*The old pannierway,
East Arncliff Wood*

At the rail station, Beggar's Bridge is hidden behind the low viaduct: pass under it to view the old bridge then return to leave the road immediately by a footbridge over Glaisdale Beck to enter East Arncliff Wood. The path climbs steeply, nears the river, and soon climbs again on a lengthy paved section. A gentler finish leads out onto a quiet road: turn downhill towards Egton Bridge. At a T-junction just past the Horseshoe the way keeps on to the road bridge over the River Esk, but a nicer option goes down steps to the river (under a footbridge), where dependable stepping-stones cross it in two stages, latterly beneath a millpond. Up onto the road, turn right to a junction between the church and the road bridge (Egton Bridge itself). Depart by the enclosed way almost opposite, signed 'Egton Estates - private road'.

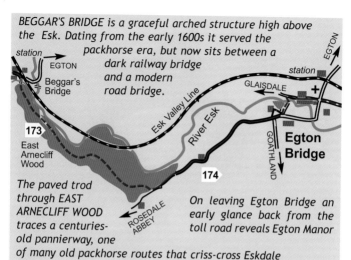

BEGGAR'S BRIDGE is a graceful arched structure high above the Esk. Dating from the early 1600s it served the packhorse era, but now sits between a dark railway bridge and a modern road bridge.

station
EGTON
Beggar's Bridge
EGTON
station
GLAISDALE
Egton Bridge
GOATHLAND
Esk Valley Line
River Esk
173
East Arnecliff Wood
174

The paved trod through EAST ARNECLIFF WOOD traces a centuries-old pannierway, one of many old packhorse routes that criss-cross Eskdale

ROSEDALE ABBEY

On leaving Egton Bridge an early glance back from the toll road reveals Egton Manor

EGTON BRIDGE is a fascinating little place, rich in historical, natural and cultural attractions. Neighbour of the hilltop Egton, it stands embowered in greenery in a lovely corner of Eskdale. This was the birthplace of Nicholas Postgate, 'martyr of the moors', who spent many post-Reformation decades working in this strongly Catholic district. Finally apprehended in 1679, he was hung, drawn and quartered on the Knavesmire at York, an old priest of 82. His memory is perpetuated by a village pub, and his faith by the beautiful church of St Hedda, built in 1866 and famed for its bas-relief panels set into the exterior walls. Further interest is found in the gooseberry show, held every August for two centuries. The toll road is another fine tradition - although the charges affixed to the cottage no longer apply. Always, at Egton Bridge, there is of course the Esk itself, a famous salmon river and the National Park's major watercourse.

Panel at St Hedda's church, Egton Bridge

141

On the old Egton Bridge toll road

The River Esk at Grosmont

BARNARDS ROAD TOLL

1 HORSE 2 WHEELS			4ᴰ
2	"	4 "	8ᴰ
2	"	4 "	8ᴰ
3	"	"	1'-
MOTOR CAR 4 "			1'-
"	3 "		1'-
MOTOR CYCLE SIDE CAR			1'-
MOTOR LORRY			2'-
MOTOR BUS			3'-
TRACTOR			1'-
HEARSE			6ᴰ

THIS GATE IS CLOSED AND LOCKED
AT 10ᴘᴍ DAILY

EGTON ESTATES OFFICE
AUG 1948

The old toll road runs unfailingly along the floor of Eskdale - passing the surviving tollhouse - to emerge onto a road on the edge of Grosmont. Turn right over the sturdy bridge to enter the village, and along to the level crossing in the centre.

First encountered at Beggar's Bridge, and sharing a similar valley-bottom course to you as far as Grosmont, is the ESK VALLEY LINE. A miracle survivor of Dr Beeching's axe, this railway bears the hallmark of a true rural line of several decades past. More importantly, the Middlebrough-Whitby railway is a lifeline to the communities along its route, in a valley that does not readily take to buses. Chasing the Esk through the winding dale floor, it bridges the river on no less than 18 occasions.

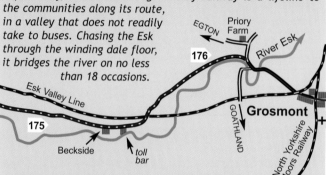

GROSMONT (pronounced 'Grow-mont' - as in Bill Beaumont) is a pleasant village firmly embedded at the foot of numerous steep roads. Dominated in the 19th century by ironstone mining (of which scars remain) there is less to see of earlier times, when - as Grosmond - it supported an abbey of the little known Grandmontine order. Dissolved in 1536, Priory Farm now occupies the site. Earlier still, a Roman fort existed in the neighbourhood. Today railways take centre stage, for here the Esk Valley Line meets the privately operated North Yorkshire Moors Railway, each with its own station. The Whitby-Pickering Railway opened in 1836 as a horse-drawn tramway, and a decade later was improved to take locomotives. The section south of Grosmont closed in 1965, only to be saved by enthusiasts and re-opened (initially to Goathland) in 1973. Today visitors can enjoy a steam-hauled 18 miles run to Pickering through the heart of the moors - a memorable trip - and now to Whitby itself. Grosmont has several tearooms as well as the Station Tavern and Crossing Club, also a Post office/store and a second-hand bookshop.

16

GROSMONT TO ROBIN HOOD'S BAY

DISTANCE 15^{1}2 miles (25km)   *ASCENT 1720 feet/525m*

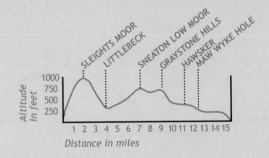

This final stage is an extravaganza of variety, leaving the steam trains behind for ancient burial mounds, heather moors, an idyllic hamlet, a beautiful waterfall in glorious woodland, and last but not least an exhilarating clifftop. The stage begins with a concerted pull onto Sleights Moor while you're still fresh: the intervening valley of Littlebeck is a delight, and one last ascent takes you onto the walk's final tract of moorland. The clifftop finale is one that will remain with you when you set off for home: it's a classic no matter what state you're in! With a Grosmont, rather than Glaisdale, start, you should hopefully be able to finish in a condition to undertake the ritual celebrations.

The wayward lurching of the route is such that if you've bitten off too much, there are opportunities to omit sections. These include an old pannier way from Grosmont along the valley side to Sleights, and if desperate clinging to the valley floor to taste salt-water at Whitby, or cross from Sleights to Sneaton and pick up the route at Hawsker. Easier finishes are a direct march from Graystone Hills, or a brisk walk along the old railway instead of the clifftop (this saves little, but misses a lot).

Depart Grosmont by simply going straight on up the street climbing out, ignoring two branches left (both for Whitby via Sleights). When the road breaks onto the open moor things start to relent, passing un-noticed the Low Bride Stones and levelling out to see the far more conspicuous High Bride Stones.

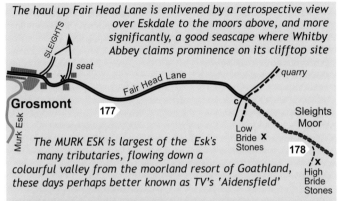

The haul up Fair Head Lane is enlivened by a retrospective view over Eskdale to the moors above, and more significantly, a good seascape where Whitby Abbey claims prominence on its clifftop site

SLEIGHTS

seat

Fair Head Lane

quarry

Grosmont

177

Sleights Moor

Murk Esk

Low Bride Stones

178

The MURK ESK is largest of the Esk's many tributaries, flowing down a colourful valley from the moorland resort of Goathland, these days perhaps better known as TV's 'Aidensfield'

High Bride Stones

Though extensively damaged, the BRIDE STONES were originally circles at least 30 feet in diameter. Whilst the Low Bride Stones skulk insignificantly in a reedy patch, their bigger cousins occupy a more open aspect, and though fewer are far more noteworthy.

Steam at Grosmont

High Bride Stones

FLAT HOWE is a round barrow in a kerb of retaining stones - heather entirely covers it. Arousing greater enthusiasm for you, however, as you cross Sleights Moor, is the wide sweep of coastline in view. Whitby is revealed in near-entirety: it's a long time since you were near anywhere that size. Coincidentally enough, its relationship with Robin Hood's Bay is not dissimilar to that between Whitehaven and St Bees. Remember St Bees?

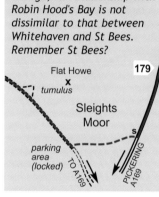

This line of upright stones is a former sheepfold

Flat Howe
x
tumulus

179

g

x x x
butts

g/s

WHITBY A169
Blue Bank

SLEIGHTS

Sleights Moor

s

parking area (locked)

TO A169

PICKERING A169

The long descent to Littlebeck offers wide views over the woods and down to the Esk

Descending from Sleights Moor to Littlebeck

Beyond the High Bride Stones take a path left through the heather opposite a parking area. This drops gently to soon reach a stile in a fence enclosing the A169. Cross with care and go left along the capacious verge towards the top of Blue Bank. After five minutes a bridle-gate sends a little path the short way along to join a broad track descending from the road. Turn down this as it descends the moor, leaving heather for bracken before joining a stony track for the last few steps down to the head of a surfaced lane. With its central grassy strip continue the descent to a through road, and maintain the long descent still further as this drops down into the sylvan setting of Littlebeck.

Over either ford or footbridge climb the road only as far as the second bend, where a kissing-gate on the right leads into the woods. A good path heads upstream, becoming temporarily diverted from Little Beck by a waterfall on a small tributary.

The hamlet of LITTLEBECK is a little corner of heaven. A surviving Methodist chapel and a converted mill augment the many natural attractions, which include a nature reserve in Littlebeck Wood. And it's the gateway to Falling Foss: you'll like Falling Foss.

Falling Foss, Littlebeck

Beyond a spoilheap (former alum quarry) continue on before climbing steeply to the Hermitage. Leave by the main (upper) path, and when it quickly forks take the right branch, slanting down by a wall before running to a fork. Keep right to enjoy a fine terraced section before descending to a viewpoint above Falling Foss: just beyond is a tearoom. From the adjacent footbridge cross a farm road and head upstream. Within a minute the path fords the beck to lead upstream to a bridge at May Beck car park.

Turn up the road doubling back left, until just past the sharp bend above New May Beck Farm. A grassy track strikes off over Sneaton Low Moor, quickly turning left to become a narrower path through heather. Ahead, the B1416 is heard and then seen long before it is joined. Turning right, a well-tramped verge offers pleasanter progress along this well-used road.

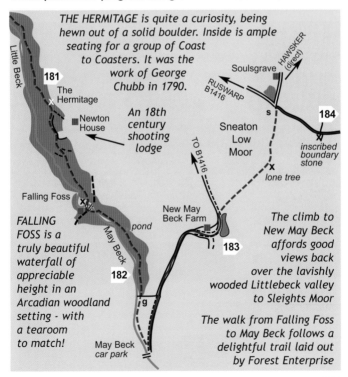

THE HERMITAGE is quite a curiosity, being hewn out of a solid boulder. Inside is ample seating for a group of Coast to Coasters. It was the work of George Chubb in 1790.

Little Beck

181

The Hermitage

Newton House

An 18th century shooting lodge

HAWSKER (direct)

Soulsgrave

RUSWARP B1416

s

184

Sneaton Low Moor

TO B1416

inscribed boundary stone

x lone tree

Falling Foss

FALLING FOSS is a truly beautiful waterfall of appreciable height in an Arcadian woodland setting - with a tearoom to match!

New May Beck Farm

pond

May Beck

182

183

The climb to New May Beck affords good views back over the lavishly wooded Littlebeck valley to Sleights Moor

9

May Beck car park

The walk from Falling Foss to May Beck follows a delightful trail laid out by Forest Enterprise

149

Before too long a gate/stile on the other side of the road give access to the great heathery tract of Graystone Hills. With a seascape ahead again, another clear path heads away for a grand stroll well away from the busy A171 to the right. Happily this road is avoided as the path swings further north to cling tenaciously to a final march of heather. With the culmination of moorland walking just ahead, a fork is reached not far beyond a small mire: keep right here, this leads happily to a boardwalk across a much more substantial marsh. On the other side is a very pleasant amble past gorse to the end of the moor.

Through the gate/stile the initially faint way drops between rampant gorse bushes to a gate in the bottom corner. Now enclosed by exuberant hedgerows, a slim path descends Middle Rigg to emerge onto the sharp bend of a back road. Continue downhill, then at a junction turn right for Hawsker.

The path on Middle Rigg

The first sign....

HAWSKER |
ROBIN HOOD'S BAY 3½
SCARBOROUGH 18½

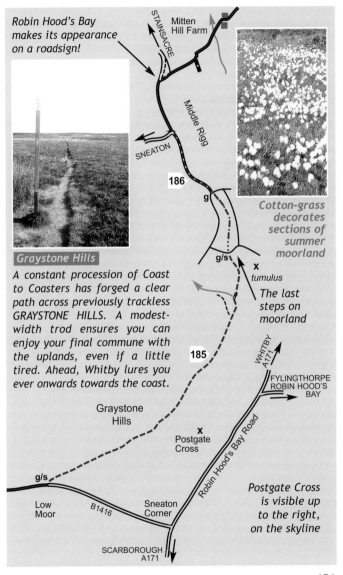

Robin Hood's Bay makes its appearance on a roadsign!

STAINSACRE

Mitten Hill Farm

Middle Rigg

SNEATON

186

g

g/s

Graystone Hills

A constant procession of Coast to Coasters has forged a clear path across previously trackless GRAYSTONE HILLS. A modest-width trod ensures you can enjoy your final commune with the uplands, even if a little tired. Ahead, Whitby lures you ever onwards towards the coast.

Cotton-grass decorates sections of summer moorland

x tumulus

The last steps on moorland

WHITBY A171

FYLINGTHORPE ROBIN HOOD'S BAY

185

Graystone Hills

x Postgate Cross

Robin Hood's Bay Road

g/s

Low Moor

B1416

Sneaton Corner

SCARBOROUGH A171

Postgate Cross is visible up to the right, on the skyline

The Robin Hood's Bay coastline, at last!

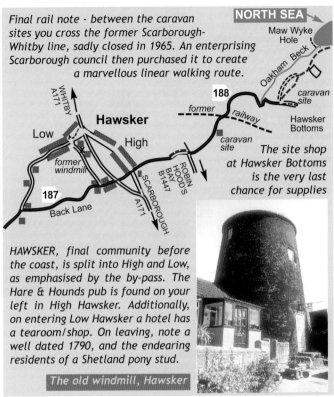

Final rail note - between the caravan sites you cross the former Scarborough-Whitby line, sadly closed in 1965. An enterprising Scarborough council then purchased it to create a marvellous linear walking route.

NORTH SEA

Maw Wyke Hole

Oakham Beck

188

former railway

WHITBY A171

Hawsker

Low

High

former windmill

187

Back Lane

ROBIN HOOD'S BAY B1447

SCARBOROUGH A171

caravan site

Hawsker Bottoms

caravan site

The site shop at Hawsker Bottoms is the very last chance for supplies

caravan site

HAWSKER, final community before the coast, is split into High and Low, as emphasised by the by-pass. The Hare & Hounds pub is found on your left in High Hawsker. Additionally, on entering Low Hawsker a hotel has a tearoom/shop. On leaving, note a well dated 1790, and the endearing residents of a Shetland pony stud.

The old windmill, Hawsker

Keep straight on and along the edge of Low Hawsker to cross the A171 before entering the village street. Continue out along the Robin Hood's Bay road (initially with a footway, then parallel path on left), and when it swings right keep straight on Bottoms Lane, past one caravan site (Seaview) and down to a second (Northcliffe). Just past the shop/tearoom the road ends, and here descend the right-hand site road through the caravans, continuing down as a path takes over to meet the coast path above Maw Wyke Hole, and thus, after a long absence, the Cleveland Way. This is indeed a classic moment: reaching the coast is sufficiently thrilling, but the grandeur of the scenery makes it doubly satisfying. Turn right to savour the final miles.

This stirring finale is distinctly obvious as it is bounded on one side by majestic cliffs and the North Sea. On eventually rounding Ness Point just beneath a coastguard lookout, Robin Hood's Bay comes fully into view, and the village itself is soon within your sights. Beyond Rocket Post Field a gate at last leads into Arcadian greenery to emerge onto a residential street, Mount Pleasant North. At the end turn left to descend the bustling main street all the way down through the heart of the village - to its inevitable conclusion. Keep on out onto the stony shore, just as far as the North Sea happens to be, and that's it, you've done it!

Journey's end, rainbow's end.....
.... Robin Hood's Bay

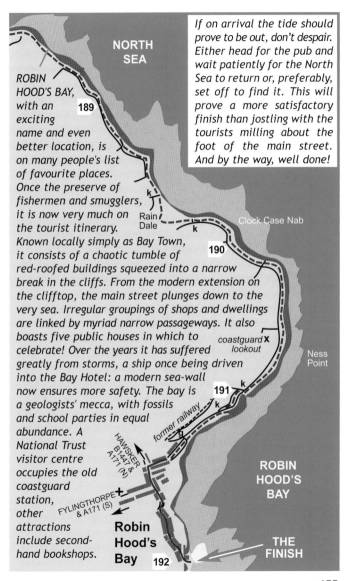

NORTH SEA

ROBIN HOOD'S BAY, with an 189 exciting name and even better location, is on many people's list of favourite places. Once the preserve of fishermen and smugglers, it is now very much on the tourist itinerary. Known locally simply as Bay Town, it consists of a chaotic tumble of red-roofed buildings squeezed into a narrow break in the cliffs. From the modern extension on the clifftop, the main street plunges down to the very sea. Irregular groupings of shops and dwellings are linked by myriad narrow passageways. It also boasts five public houses in which to celebrate! Over the years it has suffered greatly from storms, a ship once being driven into the Bay Hotel: a modern sea-wall now ensures more safety. The bay is a geologists' mecca, with fossils and school parties in equal abundance. A National Trust visitor centre occupies the old coastguard station, other attractions include second-hand bookshops.

If on arrival the tide should prove to be out, don't despair. Either head for the pub and wait patiently for the North Sea to return or, preferably, set off to find it. This will prove a more satisfactory finish than jostling with the tourists milling about the foot of the main street. And by the way, well done!

Rain Dale

Clock Case Nab

190

coastguard **x** lookout

Ness Point

191

former railway

HAWSKER B1447 & A171 (N)

FLYINGTHORPE & A171 (S)

ROBIN HOOD'S BAY

Robin Hood's Bay 192

THE FINISH

RECORD OF THE JOURNEY

Date	Place	Miles daily	total	Notes
	St Bees	-	-	
	Sandwith	5	5	
	Cleator	9	9	
	Dent	11	11	
	Ennerdale Bridge	14½	14½	
	Gillerthwaite	5¼	19¾	
	Black Sail Hut	9	23½	
	Honister Pass	11¾	26¼	
	Seatoller	13¼	27¾	
	Rosthwaite	14½	29	
	Stonethwaite	1	30	
	Greenup Edge	3¾	32¾	
	Easedale	8	37	
	Grasmere	9	38	
	Grisedale Tarn	3¾	41¾	
	Patterdale	8½	46½	
	Angle Tarn	2	48½	
	Kidsty Pike	5	51½	
	Haweswater	6¾	53¼	
	Burnbanks	11	57½	
	Rosgill Bridge	2	59½	
	Shap	5	62½	
	Oddendale	7¾	65¼	
	Orton	13¼	70¾	
	Sunbiggin Tarn	3¾	74½	
	Smardale Bridge	8½	79¼	
	Waitby junction	10½	81¼	
	Kirkby Stephen	12¾	83½	
	Hartley	¾	84¼	
	9 Standards Rigg	4½	88	
	Raven Seat	9	92½	
	Keld	12	95½	

RECORD OF THE JOURNEY

Date	Place	Miles daily	total	Notes
	Gunnerside Gill	3$\frac{1}{2}$	99	
	Surrender Bridge	7$\frac{1}{4}$	102$\frac{3}{4}$	
	Reeth	11	106$\frac{1}{2}$	
	Grinton	$\frac{3}{4}$	107$\frac{1}{4}$	
	Marrick	3	109$\frac{1}{2}$	
	Marske	6$\frac{1}{4}$	112$\frac{1}{4}$	
	Richmond	11	117$\frac{1}{2}$	
	Colburn	2$\frac{3}{4}$	120$\frac{1}{4}$	
	Catterick Bridge	5	122$\frac{1}{2}$	
	Bolton on Swale	7$\frac{1}{4}$	124$\frac{3}{4}$	
	Danby Wiske	14$\frac{3}{4}$	132$\frac{1}{4}$	
	Oaktree Hill	1$\frac{3}{4}$	134	
	Long Lane	4$\frac{1}{4}$	136$\frac{1}{2}$	
	A19	8$\frac{3}{4}$	141	
	Ingleby Cross	9$\frac{1}{4}$	141$\frac{1}{2}$	
	Beacon Hill	2$\frac{1}{2}$	144	
	Huthwaite Green	5$\frac{1}{4}$	146$\frac{3}{4}$	
	Carlton Bank	8$\frac{1}{4}$	149$\frac{3}{4}$	
	The Wainstones	11	152$\frac{1}{2}$	
	Clay Bank Top	12	153$\frac{1}{2}$	
	Round Hill	2$\frac{1}{4}$	155$\frac{3}{4}$	
	Bloworth Crossing	3$\frac{1}{2}$	157	
	Lion Inn, Blakey	9	162$\frac{1}{2}$	
	Rosedale Head	10$\frac{1}{2}$	164	
	Trough House	1$\frac{1}{2}$	166	
	Glaisdale	7$\frac{1}{2}$	172	
	Egton Bridge	10	174$\frac{1}{2}$	
	Grosmont	12$\frac{1}{2}$	176$\frac{1}{2}$	
	Littlebeck	3$\frac{1}{2}$	180	
	New May Beck	6$\frac{1}{2}$	183	
	Hawsker	11	187$\frac{1}{2}$	
	Robin Hood's Bay	15$\frac{1}{2}$	192	

RECORD OF ACCOMMODATION

Date	Address	Notes

RECORD OF PUBS VISITED

Name	Location	Notes

INDEX

Place names on the route maps

INDEX continued

INDEX continued

INDEX continued

The Hermitage, Littlebeck

THE FELLOWSHIP OF THE COAST TO C

These two pages are reserved as a special mem[...] walk, perhaps for autographs and addresses of frien[...] along the way. Even the most hermit-like of walke[...] bound to encounter some like-minded souls, and a suit[...] reminder of happy events makes a nice personal touch. If y[...] do manage to avoid human contact, then use the space for [...] important notes such as the time of your train home!

Bluebells in the heather near Bloworth Crossing